Lamp & Lily

Lamp & Lily

The Letters and Writings of
VENERABLE ANTONIETTA MEO

Translated by Becket Ghioto

"Dear Jesus, I want to be your lamp, the flame that signifies the love of the heart, and your lily that signifies the purity of the soul."

— Venerable Antonietta Meo, Letter 151

EPIGRAPH

"Antonietta Meo, a little girl known as 'Nennolina'... showed special faith, hope and charity, and likewise the other Christian virtues. Although she was a frail little girl, she managed to give a strong and vigorous Gospel witness... Her life, so simple and at the same time so important, shows that holiness is for all ages: for children and for young people, for adults and for the elderly. Every season of our life can be a good time for deciding to love Jesus seriously and to follow him faithfully. In just a few years, Nennolina reached the peak of Christian perfection that we are all called to scale; she sped down the 'highway' that leads to Jesus... You know that Antonietta now lives in God and is close to you from Heaven... Learn to know her and follow her example."

Pope Benedict XVI
To boys and girls of Catholic Action
December 20, 2007

ANTONIETTA'S STORY
THE BEGINNING

Antonietta Meo was the fourth child born to Michele and Maria Meo on December 15, 1930, in Rome, Italy. Her older brother Giovanni was born in 1919, only to die at the age of two. The following year her older sister Margarita Emilia Josefina was born. Two years after that, another older sister Carmela was born, but she also died at two-years-old. Michele and Maria had no more children after Antonietta's birth four years later. She was baptized in the Basilica di Santa Croce in Gerusalemme on the Feast of the Holy Innocents. In the years following her christening, her family began affectionately nicknaming her "Nennolina."

Her mother Maria's memoir recollects that Antonietta was a very loving child. Playfully, she would climb onto her father's knees, summon her mother and sister to come closer, position everyone's faces so that Maria and Michele faced each other while she faced her sister, then Antonietta would pull all four faces together so that everyone kissed at the same time, causing a great confusion of kisses, laughter, and joyful shouts.

At the age of three, Antonietta was enrolled in a local Catholic school run by the Daughters of Our Lady of Mount Calvary. In the following year, she was enrolled at another Catholic school near their home, run by the Zealots of the Sacred Heart—a relatively new religious order of nuns founded fifty years earlier.

During that year, Antonietta fell on the playground and bruised her left knee. She began to complain that the knee felt numb and the swelling was not diminishing. Her parents took her to the S. Stefano Rotondo's Clinic where radiography revealed that she had aggressive bone cancer. Doctors prescribed calcium injections (a common treatment for bone cancer at that time), but they were so painful that Antonietta asked her mother if they could stop. Maria reminded Antonietta about the great suffering that Jesus endured for the world, then she taught her daughter the value of uniting her suffering to the Cross of Christ. The child agreed to let the injections continue for another two months, offering her pain to Jesus, and bearing it by laughing and singing songs in the doctor's office. When the cancer worsened, doctors amputated her leg on April 25, 1936, just above the left knee.

Maria Meo also recollects in her memoir that, on the first night after the amputation, Antonietta did not stop crying until 11PM, when she turned to her father Michele and scolded him because they had not done their prayers. Antonietta tried to never complain about her suffering. In the morning, when her father was caressing her head, he asked her if she was in much pain. She told him, "Pain is like cloth. The stronger it is, the more it is worth."

Michele and Maria remained with their daughter during her painful recovery in the clinic. Upon release, Antonietta was fitted with a wooden leg that also gave her much pain. Unable to return to school for the next five months while her severed leg healed, Maria would spend an hour each day teaching Antonietta truths of the Catholic faith from the Catechism, while also taking her daughter to daily mass. In July, three months after her amputation, Antonietta expressed a desperate desire to receive her First Holy Communion. Her mother explained that a five-year-old kindergartner was two years too young to reach the customary "age of discretion" required for receiving First Communion, according to Pope Pius X's decree *Quam singulari* (1910). To receive a dispensation for early reception of the sacrament would require that Antonietta have, not necessarily a perfect understanding of Christian doctrine, but a willingness to learn Christian doctrine from the Catechism, a knowledge of salvation according to the Mysteries of Faith, and the ability to distinguish between ordinary bread and the Bread of the Most Holy Eucharist. That did nothing to diminish Antonietta's longing to receive the Eucharist; in fact, it only fanned the flame of her love for the Lord. For the next two months, Maria continued teaching Antonietta from the Catechism while Antonietta continued to express a deep need to receive the Blessed Sacrament. Two months later, when her leg had healed enough for her to return to school, Maria gave Antonietta permission to ask her school's Mother Superior if she could receive First Holy Communion early.

On the day Antonietta made the painful walk to school with her new wooden leg, a new habit also began—she commenced a correspondence with God the Father, Jesus, the Holy Spirit, and the Blessed Virgin Mother. Because she was just learning how to write, she only wrote five letters, twenty-two diary entries, and two essays, but she dictated to her mother one-hundred-fifty-seven more letters, some of which were also addressed to her family. Any reply she received from her Divine Pen-pals can only be evidenced in the letters themselves, which reveal the progress of a soul from childish to childlike. Her letters are a love story of grace in the sacraments. And they begin where all great love stories begin—with a journey. Without mentioning her severed leg or her painfully wooden prosthetic, Antonietta's very first letter informs Jesus in joyfully expressive words that she is going on a walk to ask permission to receive a very special Christmas gift—Jesus in the Eucharist.

Later that afternoon, when Antonietta returned home, her mother asked if walking to school was painful. Antonietta's reply showed her mother that even her actions were letters to Jesus of the child's profound faith: "Every step I take is a little word of love."

The Letters and Writings of Venerable Antonietta Meo

Letter 1

September 15, 1936

Dear Jesus,

Today, I'm going for a walk to the nuns and I'll tell them that I would like to make my First Communion this Christmas.

Jesus, come into my heart soon so I can hug you very tightly and kiss you!

O Jesus, I want you to stay in my heart always!

Love and a kiss from your,

Antonietta

Letter 2

September 18, 1936, Rome

Loving Jesus, I give you my heart.
Jesus, give me souls!
Jesus, you are good.
Jesus, welcome your little girl.
Kiss her, loving Jesus.

Letter 3

September 18, 1936, Rome

Mary, you are good.

Come down to us and bless us. Take my heart and bring it to Jesus.

O Mary, you are the star of our heart!

Antonietta

Letter 4

September 18, 1936

O Jesus, you are good!
O Loving Jesus, your little girl sends you a kiss.
Love to you, O Loving Jesus!

Letter 5

September 21, 1936

Dear Jesus,
My love for you is all!
Jesus, save your little girl from danger.
Give me souls. I give you my heart.

Mary, I write to you, too.
O Mary, you are always good.
Mary, in life we must:
   1. Be good
   2. Obey
   3. Make ourselves holy so we can go to Heaven.

Antonietta

Letter 6

September 22, 1936

O Baby Jesus, I love you very much!

I had a very bad little tantrum today. Forgive me. I never want to do that again.

Kisses from your,

Antonietta

Letter 7

September 22, 1936

O Jesus, you are good.
Loving Jesus, your little girl sends you a kiss!
Love to you, O Loving Jesus!

Letter 8

September 23, 1936

Dear Baby Jesus,

Give me these two graces. First, make me grow in goodness. Second, make me walk better.

O Baby Jesus, help my parents, protect them, protect my sister. O Baby Jesus, help everyone, both good and bad.

O Baby Jesus, I kiss you and I cannot wait to hug you in my heart! I have been waiting for you for a long time!

Jesus, come quickly into my heart!

Baby Jesus, bless everybody. Save them!

Jesus, give me souls.

Baby Jesus, Mother Superior says she's happy to let me make my First Communion. Thank you for giving me that grace. Baby Jesus, bless Mother Superior, all the nuns, all nuns around the world, and bless all priests!

Baby Jesus, bless poor missionaries. Bless poor unbelieving children. Baby Jesus, bless everyone in the whole world.

Thank you, and kisses from your,
Antonietta

Diary Entry 1

September 25, 1936

I stayed in bed, as mommy wanted. I did not call for my sister while mommy went out.

I obeyed mommy. Help me, so that the day when I receive you into my heart will come soon.

Letter 9

September 26, 1936

Dear Baby Jesus,

You are holy. You are good. Help me. Grant my prayer and give me back my little leg. Give me souls. Loving Jesus, don't leave my heart anymore. Be with me always.

Dear Baby Jesus, you are holy! You are good! Help me. Grant my prayer and give me back my little leg, if you want to. If you do not want to, thy will be done.

Jesus, give me souls.

Loving Jesus, do not leave my heart. Stay with me always.

Diary Entry 2

September 26, 1936

I stopped playing so that I could obey mommy. Jesus, I want to be good.

I ate all my food for love of Jesus.

Dear Jesus, I promise that I will do as much tomorrow.

Letter 10

September 27, 1936

Dear Baby Mary,

Help me. Protect me. Pray for me to Jesus that he will make me grow in goodness, Holy Mary.

O Mary, you are holy!

Diary Entry 3

September 26, 1936

I obeyed for love of Jesus.
Jesus, I send you a kiss.

I am being good while mommy goes to church.
Jesus, my mercy.

I did not eat candy until I said my prayers.
My Jesus, I send you love.

Letter 11

September 28, 1936

To Mommy,
Mommy, you are a sweet, lovely rose.
Mommy, you are love!
Mommy, I bless you.
Mommy, O Sweet Love, I bless your heart.
Mommy, I kiss the bright flower that you are, O
Sweet Love.
Mommy, you care for your children who bless you.
Mommy, you are very good. Oh, how good you are!
O Mommy, sweet love, I just kiss the rose.

Letter 12

September 28, 1936

Dear Daddy,

Best wishes from your Nennolina! O Loving Daddy, your little girl kisses you and blesses your heart.

Daddy, you are good, and you want so much goodness for your Nennolina, who always prays for you, and tells Jesus to give you health and to make you go to Heaven, but first to give you many more years of life.

These are the wishes of your Nennolina.

Letter 13

September 28, 1936

Daddy,
Daddy, O Sweet Love,
I bless you and kiss your heart.
I kiss you all over, O Sweet Love.
You are the father of your little girls.
You are good. You are love.
O Daddy, the rose in your hand smells sweetest.

Letter 14

September 28, 1936

To Margherita,
Margherita, you are good to walk with me.
O Dear Sister, a kiss to your heart.
Love to your soul!

Letter 15

September 28, 1936

To Mary,
Mary, you are always good.
Come down upon us and bless us.
Take my heart. Take it to Jesus.
Oh, Mary, you are the star of our heart!

Letter 16

September 28, 1936

To Jesus,
Loving Jesus, I give you my heart.
Jesus, give me souls!
Jesus, you are always good!
Jesus, welcome your little girl.
Kiss her, O Loving Jesus.

Letter 17

October 3, 1936

Dear Baby Jesus,

O Baby Jesus, forgive me if I have said bad prayers. You are so good!

Bless me. Bless my daddy, my mommy, my sister. Bless also my grandparents, uncles, aunts, and even Caterina.[1]

Baby Jesus, protect my daddy, my mommy, and my sister, and give them good health. Baby Jesus, help me to have good sleep. Baby Jesus, forgive all the sins I have done.

Baby Jesus, give everyone good health. Bless priests and unbelievers. And reveal yourself to bad people who do not want to know you.

Baby Jesus, I bless you and kiss you with all my heart!

Baby Jesus, give me souls!

Good night, Jesus.

Good night, Mary.

Many kisses from your,

Antonietta

---

[1] Caterina is the family nanny, and often mothered Antonietta alongside Maria Meo.

Letter 18

October 3, 1936

Dear Jesus,

I ask you to forgive all the sins I have done today.

Dear baby Jesus, I love you so much. Today I did every possible thing to make you happy. Bless everyone in the whole world, priests, unbelievers, and bless my parents.

Many kisses from your,

Antonietta

Letter 19

October 4, 1936

Dear Mary,

You are so good. Help us, protect us, save us. You too, Jesus!

Mary, help me to be good so that I can make a good and holy Communion.

Mary, bless us, save my daddy, save my mommy, save good and bad people. Help my daddy. Protect the whole world!

Mary, protect my sister whom I love very much. Dear Mary, pray to Jesus to make me grow in goodness. Bless all nuns, priests, missionaries, and unbelievers.

Many kisses from your,

Antonietta

Letter 20

October 4, 2036

Dear St. Thérèse,[2]
I love you so much. Please pray to Jesus that I will be good.
Many kisses from your,
Antonietta

---

[2] Antonietta addressed the letter to "S. Teresina" only, without specifying "Lisieux." However, it is highly likely that she is in fact writing to St. Thérèse of Lisieux—and not another popular saint by that name, such as Teresa of Avila—because the Italian culture refers to the saint both as Santa Teresa di Lisieux or simply Santa Teresina (Little Thérèse). It is also highly likely that she is referring to Saint Thérèse of Lisieux on the testimony of Antonietta's mother, Maria, who confessed that, on the day of Antonietta's death, despite her great suffering, Antonietta wanted to remain and suffer a few more days, but Saint Thérèse of Lisieux appeared and told her, "It is enough."

Letter 21

October 4, 1936

Dear Jesus,
I love you very much. I pray to you so that you will make me good.
Many kisses from your,
Antonietta

Letter 22

October 5, 1936

Dear Jesus,

I dedicate every day to you and to your mommy. I will always find you in church and say Hi to you, your mommy, and the good saints.

O Dear Jesus, give me souls and make them become good. Make many souls grow in goodness.

O Dear Baby Jesus, you are so good. Forgive me and all children. Help unbelieving children to know you.

Loving Baby Jesus, I want to always be good because you make souls grow in goodness. Make many become good!

O Baby Jesus, I have been waiting for you for so long in my heart. I just can't wait for Christmas! Truly, Christmas is the most beautiful day! It's beautiful because I want to receive you into my heart.

Many blessings and kisses for you and for your mommy from your,

Antonietta

Letter 23

October 8, 1936

Dear Baby Jesus,

I want to apologize for what I did.

Baby Jesus, you are so good. Forgive me. I promise I will not be mean to Margherita.

O Baby Jesus, you are so good. Forgive everyone. Baby Jesus, you are always good. Also, forgive my mommy. Baby Jesus, you are always good. Forgive my daddy. And also forgive my sister. I love her so much! Jesus, I can't wait to hold you!

Baby Jesus, many kisses from your Antonietta, who loves you very much!

Baby Jesus, come with me to school. I really like going there. Bless my teacher. She loves children.[3]

Kisses from your,

Antonietta

---

[3] Records of Antonietta's teacher at this age are irretrievable, but she mentions two names as her teacher, Sister Noemi in Letters 33 and 57, and Sister Bertolina in Letters 34 and 37. It is possible that she had two teachers Sister Noemi and Sister Bertolina, or it is more likely these names refer to one religious teacher, Sister Noemi Bertolina.

Letter 24

Dear Baby Jesus,

Today, I want to be very good at school and never disobey my teacher.

Dear Baby Jesus, I love you very much, and I want you to be near me always because of how much I love you!

Dear Baby Jesus, come to school with me and bless everyone. Bless my teacher. She loves children!

Baby Jesus, make Christmas come soon! I'm waiting for you and I want to receive you.

Love and caresses from your child,
Antonietta

Letter 25

October 9, 1936

Dear Baby Mary,

Help me. Protect me. Pray for me to Jesus to make me be good.

Holy Mary!

O Mary! You are holy!

Jesus, you are holy! You are good. Loving Jesus, do not leave my heart any more. Stay with me always.

Letter 26

October 9, 1936

Dear Jesus,
I love you so much. O Jesus, you are always so
good. Help me and forgive all the sins that I have done.
Many kisses from your,
Antonietta

Letter 27

October 9, 1936

Dear Baby Jesus,

I love you very much! Baby Jesus, help me. Protect me.

O Baby Jesus, give me souls. Come quickly into my heart. O Loving Baby Jesus, O Baby Jesus, I kiss you.

O Baby Jesus, make the Mother Superior agree to let my teacher prepare me to make First Holy Communion.[4]

Baby Jesus, help my parents. Baby Jesus, help my sister. Baby Jesus, help everyone. Save us. Protect us from danger.

A kiss from your Antonietta who loves you.

---

[4] As with the note for letter 23, the teacher Antonietta is referring to could be Sister Noemi, Sister Bertolina, or Sister Noemi Bertolina. Regardless, her teacher is a religious, and needs the permission of the Mother Superior to allow her students to receive First Communion.

Letter 28

October 12, 1936

Dear Baby Jesus,

Thank you for letting me go to mass yesterday. I was very good in church because the church is your home.

O Baby Jesus, I love you so much and I want you to be near me always, especially tomorrow, when school begins. I gladly go to school because we learn many beautiful things about you and your saints.

O Baby Jesus, give me souls because I love you very much. I wish everyone wanted to love you so much too.

Jesus, come quickly. My heart has been waiting for you for so long.

A kiss from your,
Antonietta

Letter 29

October 15, 1936

Dear Baby Jesus,

I hope that we will soon begin learning the Catechism in my school, but I already know a little. Hopefully by Christmas, I'll know it better, so I can receive you worthily into my heart.

Dear Baby Jesus, I love you very much! Bless everyone, especially my parents, grandparents, and my sister whom I love very much.

Dear Baby Jesus, I will be good and do many little flowers[5] and give them to you at my First Holy Communion.

Blessings and kisses from your, Nennolina

Good night, Jesus!

Good night, Mary!

Jesus, I entrust my grandparents to you.

---

[5] Antonietta's word for "little flowers" (*fioretti*) is also in the title *Fioretti di San Francesco* (The Little Flowers of St. Francis), written around 1322. Because that book is mostly a compilation of the acts of Saint Francis and his companions, "fioretti" does not simply mean the "little flowers" of a field, but also the corporal good works blossoming on the meadow of the soul. In other words, Antonietta's *little flowers* are her *little sacrifices*. Antonietta's mother also uses this same word in her memoir when relating how Antonietta's kindergarten teacher, Sister Noemi, explained how Antonietta made innumerable "i sacrifici e i fioretti"—literally, "sacrifices and little flowers;" but more accurately, *sacrifices and little sacrifices*.

Letter 30

October 15, 1936

Dear Mary,

I love you very much! You are so good! You are the mommy of the world, of all good and bad people. Help me to be good and not to have temper tantrums. Pray to Jesus to bless the whole world, my parents, and my sister whom I love very much, but I love you and Jesus more.

Dear Mary, I want to be very good, to convert people who do not love Jesus, so pray to Jesus to give me souls.

Dear Mary, help me to do many little flowers that I will give to Jesus when I make my First Holy Communion.

O Mary, I send you love and a kiss!

Your loving daughter,

Antonietta

Letter 31

October 16, 1936

Dear Mary,

I love you very much! You are so good!

You are the mommy of the world, of all people, the good and the bad. Help me to make amends for people's sins, especially the really bad ones.

Jesus in the Eucharist, your Antonietta loves you and kisses you.

Good night, Jesus!

Good night, Mary!

Letter 32

Dear Baby Jesus,

I love you so very much! Yes, I know that you are very good and that no one is as good as you. Tomorrow morning, if I can, I will go to Mass to come find you.

Dear baby Jesus, make me walk better. Forgive everyone, forgive good and bad people, forgive my parents, and my sister whom I love so much, though I love you most.

O Baby Jesus, I love you very much and I cannot wait to hold you! Yes, it is true, I have not done any little flowers today, but tomorrow I will do many and make up for today.

Baby Jesus, you know I love my school very much. I would even go at night! I like it because they teach the truth about you and the Catechism, to prepare me for my First Holy Communion!

Many blessings and kisses from your dear,
Antonietta

Letter 33

October 16, 1936

Dear Jesus in the Eucharist,

I love you so much—no, really very much!—not just because you are the father of the whole world, but also because you are the whole world's King! I want to be the little lamp that burns night and day in front of you and near you in the Sacrament.

Jesus, I want to ask you for three graces. First, make me holy because that's the most important thing. Second, give me souls. Third, make me walk better, but this is really not very important. I'm not telling you to give me back my leg because I've already given that to you.

Jesus in the Eucharist, I really like my teacher, Sister Noemi. I love her dearly. Help her to do all necessary things that you want her to do.

Dear Jesus in the Eucharist, I love you so much. I cannot wait for Christmastime to come! When you come into my poor heart, make my heart burn with lots of light for you!

Dear Jesus, I want to make many sacrifices for you to offer to you when I make my First Holy Communion.

Dear Jesus in the Eucharist, I want to suffer a lot, to make amends for people's sins, especially for those who are very bad.

Jesus in the Eucharist, your Antonietta loves you and kisses you.

Good night, Jesus.

Good night, Mary.

Letter 34

October 17, 1936

Dear Baby Jesus,

I love you very much. Help my teacher, Sister Bertolina, because she is very good.

Dear baby Jesus, help me. I hope that Christmas comes soon because I want to receive you into my heart!

Dear baby Jesus, help my parents and my sister whom I love very much, but not as much as I love you.

Dear baby Jesus, today I got a medal because I was good!

You know, baby Jesus, I really like school.

Many blessings and kisses from your,

Antonietta

Letter 35

October 18, 1936

Dear Baby Jesus,
I love you very much!

Truthfully, I was a little bad last night, but I promise to never do it again because I want to prepare to make my First Holy Communion.

Dear Baby Jesus, I love you so much! I gladly went to mass today.

Dear Baby Jesus, protect me, save me from every danger in the world and in this city.

Dear Jesus, I got a medal yesterday! Help my parents, my sister, and the missions. I pray a lot for the missions, that you will bring all missionaries home safely, and that they win many souls, even the bad ones.

Jesus, bless all priests.

Dear Jesus, make Christmas come soon so I can receive you into my heart!

Blessings from your dear Antonietta…and also kisses!

Letter 36

October 19, 1936

Dear Baby Jesus,

I hope to receive you soon in Holy Communion. Help my teacher, Sister Bartolina. And make me very good so that one day I can be with you in Heaven.

Dear Baby Jesus, do you know that my daddy is sick? Heal him. Help mommy too.

Dear Baby Jesus, help all priests and all nuns.

Dear Jesus, give me souls, and heal me so I can go back to school.

Kisses and blessings from your,

Antonietta

Letter 37

October 19, 1936

Dear Jesus,

I love you very much. Thank you for healing my daddy. Help my mommy too. Also, protect Sister Bertolina and my sister and all priests and nuns.

I hope Christmas comes soon!

Dear Jesus, save me from all dangers.

Blessings and kisses,

Antonietta

Letter 38

Dear Baby Jesus,

Because I love you so much, I hope that I can receive you soon in First Holy Communion. Dear Jesus, to receive you properly in Holy Communion, when you come into my heart, I would like it to be full of little flowers and light.

Dear Jesus, this morning, I went to church and I was very happy because I came to see you, and also because I wanted to hear the many beautiful words that the priest spoke of you.

Dear Jesus, to make you happy, I would like to have many souls.

Last night I did not write to you, but tonight I am writing you a long, beautiful letter, to tell you many beautiful things that will make you happy.

Dear Jesus, protect my mommy and my daddy and my sister whom I love very much. Dear Jesus, protect priests and missionaries, and make poor unbelievers know you.

Dear Jesus, forgive me and my sister because we were a little bad. I promise that I will be much better tomorrow. Dear baby Jesus, make me good so that one day I can be with you in Heaven. Save me from all dangers.

What a beautiful day Christmas Day will be! I hope to receive you soon. Dear baby Jesus, tell your mommy to help me be good, so I can receive you worthily into my heart.

Blessings and kisses from your dear,

Antonietta

Letter 39

October 23, 1936

Dear Jesus in the Eucharist,

I hope that Christmas will come soon so I can receive you in Holy Communion. Help me bear sorrowful pains with great patience so that I can make many little flowers to give you when I receive you in Holy Communion.

Dear Jesus, thank you for stopping the war in Africa. Make the one in Spain end too.[6]

Dear Jesus, give me souls, forgive everyone in the world, and also in Spain.

Dear Jesus, today, I got an A in school, and I hope to get more, because I want to be the first in my class to please you and Mary. I would even like to please the teacher, whom I love, but I love you more![7]

---

[6] The war in Africa that Antonietta mentions is the Second Italo-Ethiopian War that lasted from October 1935 to May 1936, and resulted in the Italian annexation and occupation of Ethiopia until the end of 1941. The war in Spain that Antonietta mentions is the Spanish Civil War that lasted from July 1936 to April 1939. The situations in both countries is a source of much concern and prayer in many of Antonietta's letters. Both wars are catalysts that would usher in World War II, beginning in 1939, only three years later.

[7] For Antonietta's A grade, she used the word *lodevole*, which in the Italian grading system at that time was based on *giudizi* (judgements). Instead of A, B, C, D, and F grades, she and her classmates received *lodevole* (praiseworthy) for A, *buono*

Dear Jesus, I entrust to you Mrs. Maria, who always gives me pastries.[8]

Dear Jesus in the Eucharist, protect my daddy, my mommy, my sister, my grandparents, and also protect your Antonietta who gives you lots of kisses and blessings!

Antonietta

(good) for B, *sufficiente* (sufficient) for C, and *insufficiente* (insufficient) for F. This translation uses "A" instead of her word "*lodevole*" to clarify her meaning.

[8] The identity of Mrs. Maria remains a mystery at present since the name Maria was very common in Rome, Italy, at that time. However, one possibility is Maria Colizzi, whom Antonietta's mother mentions in her memoir. Maria Colizzi had a hernia operation and shared a room at S. Stefano Rotondo's Clinic with Antonietta when her leg was amputated. Maria Colizzi might have become a family friend at that time, especially when she overheard Antonietta's famous remark: "Pain is like cloth: The stronger it is, the more it is worth."

Letter 40

October 24, 1936

Dear Jesus in the Eucharist,
I love you very much! I am very glad that tomorrow is your feast![9] Save me from all dangers.

---

[9] Because this date, October 24, 1936, was a Saturday, the feast that Antonietta refers to was the Thirtieth Sunday in Ordinary Time.

Letter 41

October 25, 1936

Dear Jesus,

Help Mrs. Maria because she always gives me pastries and is very good to me, and I love her dearly.

Dear Jesus, also help and protect Caterina because I love her, too.

Blessings and kisses from your dear,

Antonietta

Letter 42

October 25, 1936

Dear Jesus in the Eucharist,

I hope to receive you soon in Holy Communion! I would like to receive you from the hands of Mary. Receiving you from Mary's hands would make me more worthy to receive you.

Dear Jesus, I really like school! I would even stay overnight so that I could be at school earlier and learn more than the other students. I wish to be the first in my class! And I want to study because it really makes me happy! Dear Jesus, do you know how much I love my teacher, yes, because she is good, and also because she teaches us so many things, even to read and write? Dear Jesus, protect and bless my teacher. Do all that is necessary for her.

Letter 43

October 27, 1936

Dear Jesus in the Eucharist,

I love you so much!

I threw many tantrums today, but tomorrow I will try to be good, and I will work at being good, because I hope to give you many little flowers. Dear Jesus, you are so good. Forgive my tantrums. And also forgive the sins I committed.

Dear Jesus, I hope that Christmas will come soon, so I can receive you in Holy Communion, and to tell you many beautiful things, especially to let me die before committing a mortal sin.

Blessings and kisses from your

Antonietta

Letter 44

October 29, 1936

Great Jesus,

I love you so much and I hope that Christmas will come soon, so I can receive you in Holy Communion.

Dear Jesus, I know that you suffered a lot on the cross, but I'll be good so that you will feel less pain, and also because one day I can go to Heaven to be with you and your mommy.

Dear Jesus, help my parents and the whole world. I entrust to you that sinner whom you know.[10] And I also entrust to you Caterina and my sister whom I love very much.

Dear Jesus, how beautiful that night will be when I receive you into my little heart, because it will be the first time that I receive you! And not only will it be beautiful when I receive you, dear Jesus, but it will also

---

[10] Antonietta's phrase "that sinner whom you know" is enigmatic. The identity of the sinner remains unknown. She is likely referring to someone she saw in Rome, someone she heard about, or someone whom only Jesus knows, committing a sin. She uses this phrase again in Letters 128, 130, and 156. She also uses the phrase "that person whom you know" in Letters 45, 48, 49, 55, 59, 61, 90, 105, 129, 136, and 138, which might be referring to the same sinner or to a different person, maybe a soul in need. Letter 128 illustrates more clearly how Antonietta prays for several strangers, especially those whom she witnesses committing sins.

beautify my soul. I will try to do many little flowers and I will do everything I can to please you, my Jesus.

Many kisses and blessings from your dear Antonietta who loves you so much!

P.S. Help my mommy.

Letter 45

October 30, 1936

Dear Jesus,

I love you very, very much! I really want Christmas to come quickly. I always tell you why I want it so much. You can read in these letters that I want to receive you soon.

Dear Jesus, protect and bless the whole world, my parents, and that person whom you know. I will pray a lot for that person.

Dear Jesus, I wonder how happy I will be on the day when you enter into my heart. I think you'll be happy too.

Loving kisses from your Antonietta, and many blessings.

Antonietta

Letter 46

October 31, 1936, Rome

Dear Jesus in the Eucharist,

I hope Christmas comes soon so I can receive you in Holy Communion. I will be very happy and I hope that day comes quickly. I love you so much and I cannot wait for the day when I receive you in Holy Communion.

Dear Jesus, I love the saints very much, especially, Saint Anthony and Saint Bosco and Saint Francis. Dear Saints, say a little prayer for Jesus to heal me, my daddy, my mommy, and my sister.[11]

Dear Jesus, I will come to see you and hear you at mass tomorrow. I'll be there with great devotion for my mommy and daddy's healing.

Kisses from your dear Antonietta, and blessings.

---

[11] Antonietta's excitement for the mass on the following day, the Solemnity of All Saints.

Letter 47

November 1, 1936

Dear Jesus,

I hope Christmas comes soon so I can receive you in Holy Communion. Yes, I hope Christmas comes quickly!

Dear Jesus, I love you so much and I will make many sacrifices for you.

Dear Jesus, what a beautiful day Christmas will be! It will be a beautiful day because I will be receiving you for the first time in my heart.

Dear Jesus, how beautiful is my school! We learned to read and write and many other beautiful things. I would like to go to school at night and even on holidays.

Dear Jesus, today is the Feast of All Saints. Dear Saints, you are so good. Pray to God to heal my daddy, and to help my mommy, my sister, and my teacher.

Dear Jesus, I hope Christmas does not come too late because I cannot wait to receive you!

Dear Jesus, I would like to be the lamp that burns near you day and night, so I can tell you many beautiful, loving things.

Blessings and kisses from your dear,
Antonietta

Letter 48

November 2, 1936

Dear Jesus in the Eucharist,

I love you very, very much, and I also love your mommy.

Dear Jesus, who knows when Christmas will come! I wish it would be really, really soon. You sense it in all these letters I write. I want it to come quickly so I can receive you in Holy Communion!

Dear Jesus, make all sinners convert. I also entrust to you the person whom you know.

Dear Jesus, today is the Feast of All Souls. I want to be very good and obedient so that you, O Jesus, will free many souls from Purgatory, especially Grandfather Giovanni, because I hope Grandfather Antonio has already been freed. Dear Jesus, free all souls in Purgatory. Dear Jesus, I hope that Grandfather Giovanni is in Heaven, but if he is still in Purgatory, set him free now, and I promise that I will be very good and do many sacrifices to free him.

Blessings and kisses from your
Antonietta

Letter 49

November 3, 1936

Dear Jesus in the Eucharist,

I hope that Christmas will come soon so I can make my First Communion, then I will be very happy to receive you in my heart, but I would like a grace. I wish my heart to be completely illuminated with little flowers and sacrifices to give you when you enter into my heart.

Dear Jesus, you know that I would gladly go to school because I would like to learn many things, and also because I would like to write to you by myself.

Dear Jesus, bless my parents. Help that person whom you know. Help my sister, Caterina, all parents, and Aunt Laurina and make her little pains pass. Make the pain pass from grandma's leg. And help my teacher because I love her. Dear Jesus, give my mommy peace.

Dear Jesus, I bless you lots and I send many kisses.
Antonietta

Letter 50

November 3, 1936

Dear Jesus in the Eucharist,

I love you very much, and I pray that you always preserve the grace in my soul and the health in my body, but most importantly the grace in my soul.

Dear Jesus, who knows when that blessed day of Christmas will come, so I can receive you into my little heart, which is great in love.

Dear Jesus, I go back to school tomorrow. I have been on vacation for four days and I did everything that the teacher gave me to do.

Blessings and kisses from your dear, affectionate,
Antonietta

Letter 51

November 4, 1936

Dear Daddy,

I love you very much! I pray a lot to Jesus that he will heal you. Pray also for me, dear daddy, that I will always get better.

You know, dear daddy, I am very happy that Jesus sent me this difficulty. At least it makes me Jesus's most beloved.

Dear daddy, if you die first, pray that I will go to Heaven. But I will pray that Jesus makes you come to Heaven if I die first.

Dear daddy, I will pray a lot that Jesus gives you health and that he protects you.

Many blessings and kisses from your

Nennolina

Letter 52

Dear Jesus in the Eucharist,

I hope that Christmas will come soon so I can make my First Communion.

Dear Jesus, I love you very much! Bless my parents and heal my daddy. Bless my sister and also my grandma.

Dear Jesus, help Sister Rachele, help Caterina, and help the whole world.

Dear Jesus, who knows how beautiful that day will be when I receive you for the first time! I will be very happy to hug you tightly in my heart and tell you many things. First, I will ask for the grace to be good and to love you. Second, I'll ask you to give peace to the world. Third, I'll ask to walk better. Now, in this letter I ask for three graces, but when I receive you into my heart, I will ask for many graces.

Dear Jesus, many blessings and kisses from your Antonietta

Letter 53

November 6, 1936

Dear Jesus in the Eucharist,

I love you very much, but today I told a lie and I want to be forgiven. I ask you to forgive me with all my heart because I feel great sorrow.

Dear Jesus, who knows when Christmas will come! I am waiting with all my heart to make Holy Communion.

You know, dear Jesus, that today I began preparing to make Holy Communion. I did not learn much because I already knew so much, but the teacher taught and explained to me three questions from the Catechism.

Dear Jesus, who knows how beautiful the Holy Day of Christmas will be, when I am able to hold you in my little heart for the first time, and tell you many beautiful things! The first thing I'll ask is for you to make me holy, because that is the most important thing, along with many other things that I do not know now, but I'll know that day. I'll also pray for many people, and that you accept my prayers, O Dear Jesus.

Dear Jesus, I would like to receive from the hands of your mommy.

Dear Jesus, help my parents, make them well, and make everyone well, especially my sister, and the man I entrust to you.

Make grandma's pains pass away. And when the time comes, give her a good death. But dear Jesus, give me this grace, that grandma will live a long time.

Dear Jesus, you already know that I really like school. I learned many beautiful things today. Little by little, I am learning to read and write, so I can write to you by myself.

Many blessings and kisses from your dear,
Antonietta

Letter 54

November 7, 1936

Dear Jesus,

I love you very much! Who knows when this Holy, Blessed Christmas will come, so I can receive you into my heart!

Dear Jesus, I wonder how happy I will be this Christmas when I receive you into my little heart for the first time.

Dear Jesus, help my parents, protect my sister, bless the whole world, and bless me. Also, help my grandma, Caterina, and my aunt.

Dear Jesus, thank you for stopping the war.[12] That makes me very happy.

Dear Jesus, many blessings and kisses!

Antonietta

---

[12] Antonietta might be referring once more to the ending of the Second Italo-Ethiopian War. Alternatively, the end of the war might also be a reference to the beginning of the Axis Powers, which Mussolini announced one week earlier, on November 1, 1936. From the perspective of a child of a conservative middle class family, the alliance between Italy, Germany, and Japan might have been perceived as an end of instability amid an increasingly unstable Europe.

Letter 55

November 7, 1936

Dear Great Jesus,

I love you very much. I will make many sacrifices so that you feel less pain on the manger straw that stung you all over your body.[13]

Dear Jesus, help me find a good confessor and let me see him soon because I would like to confess.

Dear Jesus, bless my parents, make my daddy and mommy better, help my sister, that person whom you know, grandma, and Caterina.

Dear Jesus, today I went to Mass, and I was very happy and good because it was your house.

Dear Jesus, let me die before I commit an ugly mortal sin. At least then I would be able to go to Heaven in the glory of the saints and angels.

---

[13] Antonietta only wrote "quando Tu stavi sulla paglia," literally translated as "when you were on the straw." This translation clarifies it as "manger straw" to illustrate Antonietta's meaning and anticipation of Christmas. On this note, it is interesting to point out that Antonietta does not address this letter to Gesù Bambino (Baby Jesus), who was actually on the manger straw, and to whom she addresses thirty-three of her letters, but rather she addresses this letter to Gesù Grande (Great Jesus), who suffered the stripes not of straw, but of the scourging. But she does not appear to be ignorant of the irony. Either consciously or unconsciously, in Letter 56, her next letter, she juxtaposes his newborn pain on the manger straw and his adult suffering at the scourging.

Dear Jesus, I give you my heart. Make it good and holy.

Dear Jesus, I look forward to this Christmas very much and I hope that it will come soon because I want to receive you in First Communion.

Dear Jesus, many blessings and kisses from your dear,

Antonietta

Letter 56

November 9, 1936

Dear Great Jesus,

I love you very much! Who knows when Christmas will come so I can receive you in First Communion!

Dear Jesus, I will make many sacrifices to make you happy. I will make many sacrifices to make amends for the sorrowful pains you suffered in the scourging and on the manger straw that stung you.

Dear Jesus, help my parents, my sister, Caterina and grandma, and also help my aunt, the whole world, all priests, and especially missionaries.

Dear Jesus, I hope Christmas comes soon! I wonder how beautiful that day will be when you enter into my heart for the first time.

Dear Jesus, blessings and kisses from your dear,
Antonietta

Letter 57

November 10, 1936

Dear Great Jesus,

I love you very much and I hope Christmas will come soon so I can receive you into my heart. Even now I am peacefully content and happy that you are coming into my little heart, which is great in love.

Dear Jesus, you know that today in school I got an A, and also a gift—a framed picture with an image of your mommy. Sister Noemi also gave me a bouquet of silk flowers and an image of little St. Thérèse,[14] when she was a little girl, playing in the garden with her sister!

---

[14] Similar to Letter 20, Antonietta addressed this letter to "piccola S. Teresina," once again not specifying Lisieux; and like before, it is very probable that she is writing to St. Thérèse of Lisieux for two important reasons. Firstly, in this letter, Antonietta emphasizes the littleness of the saint by referring to her as "piccola S. Teresina" (tiny little St. Thérèse), who trail-blazed a "little way" of sainthood, who often referred to herself as the "Little Flower of Jesus" (cf. Saint Thérèse de Lisieux, *The Story of a Soul*), and whose *littleness* has become greatly valued since her canonization, such as, in more recent times, by Pope St. John Paul II in his Apostolic Letter, *Divini Amoris Scientia* (October 19, 1997), highlighting her "way of spiritual childhood," by Pope Benedict XVI in his General Audience (April 6, 2011), underlining how she lived "the greatest love in the smallest things of daily life," and by Pope Francis in his General Audience (December 30, 2015), comparing her life and witness to "spiritual childhood" with the humility of the infant Jesus in the Incarnation. Secondly, although it is

Dear Jesus, bless my parents, my sister, our benefactors, and also grandma and Caterina.

Dear Jesus, blessings and kisses from your Antonietta

---

possible that the saint mentioned could be Teresa of Ávila, who had two sisters, Juana and María, this is unlikely since St. Teresa of Ávila was canonized in 1622, nearly three hundred years before Antonietta's birth. It is more likely that Antonietta is referring to Saint Thérèse of Lisieux, who was canonized in 1925, when Antonietta's sister Margherita (b. 1922) was three years old, eleven years before this letter was written, when Pope Pius XI reintroduced a custom that had been abandoned for 55-years, which was to adorn the dome of St. Peter's Basilica with candles and torches for a canonization ceremony, and which received a front page article in the *New York Times*, reporting that 60,000 people attended the ceremony, the largest crowd in over two decades, after which, in the evening, over half a million pilgrims visited St. Peter's Square (cf. Loose, *Thérèse and Lisieux*, 1996, p. 335). Thus, the popularity of St. Thérèse of Lisieux was likely very strong in Rome during Antonietta's lifetime. So it is very plausible that the image she received was of St. Thérèse playing in the garden with one of the other Martin daughters—perhaps Celine (also called Sister Geneviève of the Holy Face), who was closer to Thérèse in age. Read the footnote on Letter 20 for more details.

Letter 58

November 10, 1936

Dear Baby Mary,

I love you very much! And I will make many sacrifices to make you happy.

Dear Mary, pray to Jesus to make me grow better always.

Dear Mary, I got an A and a beautiful little image of you.

Dear Mary, many kisses from your dear,

Antonietta

Letter 59

November 11, 1936

Dear Great Jesus,

I love you very much. I said the rosary really good today with my parents.

Dear Jesus, I hope that Christmas would come soon so I can receive you into my heart for the first time. That day will be very beautiful, and I will make many sacrifices to make you feel less pain when you were scourged, when you were crucified, and even when you were on the stinging manger straw.

Dear Jesus, help my parents, bless my sister, and also my grandma and my aunt. Dear Jesus, help me, save me from danger, and make me always grow better.

Dear Jesus... Jesus, please give me three graces. First, make me grow better always, and make my soul grow ever more beautiful. Second, make my heart full of light and love when I receive you in beautiful Holy Communion. Third, help that person whom you know.

Many blessings and kisses from your

Antonietta

Letter 60

November 11, 1936

Dear Mary,

I love you very much. Tell Jesus to help my teacher and also the whole world.

Dear Mary, I wonder how beautiful that day will be when your Divine Son enters into my heart, but I would like to receive him from your holy hands. Would you do that for me?

Dear Mary, many blessings and many kisses from your dear,

Antonietta

Letter 61

Dear Great Jesus,

I love you so much! Dear Jesus, I hope that Christmas comes soon so I can receive you in Holy Communion, but you must help me be very good. Make Christmas come soon!

Dear Jesus, I will make many sacrifices to save many souls so they do not go to Purgatory.

Dear Jesus, help my parents, bless my sister, bless my aunt and grandma and make her sorrowful pains pass.

Dear Jesus, who knows how beautiful Christmas day will be, when I receive you for the first time. I will be very happy! I hope to make many sacrifices for you because I would like to make a bedroom in my heart for you, full of flowers and lilies, and a nice warm bed to keep you warm, tightly against my heart.

Dear Jesus, help that person whom you know, whom I entrust to you so much. Dear Jesus, give me many souls! I ask this of you because you make them good, and with my mortifications, you will make them grow in goodness.

Dear Jesus, let me find a good confessor.

Dear Jesus, help the whole world, and especially Sister Bartolina.

Many blessings and kisses from your
Antonietta

Letter 62

November 16, 1936

Dear Baby Jesus,

I will do many sacrifices to convert and save many souls. I will also do many sacrifices for them to know and love you. Dear Jesus, I will also do many sacrifices to free souls from Purgatory. I will always say a requiem[15] a day. Jesus, free many souls. I will pray always!

Dear Jesus, I ask for souls so that you will make these souls become good, very good!

Dear Jesus, I love you very, very much!

Dear Jesus, I hope that blessed Christmas comes very, very soon, so I can receive you in Holy Communion.

Dear Jesus, bless my parents, my sister, benefactors, grandma, and my aunt.

Dear Jesus, bless the Church and the clergy.

---

[15] Antonietta's reference to the requiem likely means the short, simple invocation for the dead. Traditionally, it is prayed at cemeteries, and it also replaces the Fatima Prayer at the conclusion of each decade of the Rosary during the month of November, which is offered for the Holy Souls in Purgatory. The Latin prayer: *Réquiem ætérnam dona eis Dómine; et lux perpétua lúceat eis. Requiéscant in pace. Amen.* The English prayer: *Eternal rest grant unto them, O Lord; and let perpetual light shine upon them. May they rest in peace. Amen.*

Dear Jesus, many blessings and kisses from your affectionate

Antonietta

Letter 63

Dear Jesus in the Eucharist,

I love you very, very much! I really like my school and I'm very happy because we're learning many beautiful things, and much about you! Do you know, dear Jesus, that I began Catechism?

Dear Jesus, tell your mommy that I love her too.

Dear Jesus, give me souls! I ask you very willingly, so give me many! I ask you so that you will make them grow in goodness. I am very happy that you make them grow in goodness because I would like them all to go to Heaven with you. Especially help that man I have entrusted to you.

Dear Jesus, when will Christmas come? I have been wishing it to come for many days! True, there are still many more days till Christmas, but I would like it to be today. This I wish very much.

Dear Jesus, on the day of my First Communion, I will ask for many graces. Now, I know of only three, but on that day I shall ask for many. Let me tell you these three now... First, make me grow in goodness. Second, make me go to Heaven. Third, make me walk better. And I also ask for another, that you help my parents and my sister to go to Heaven.

Dear Jesus, bless my parents and my sister, and bless the Church and the clergy, and everyone I know.

Many blessings and kisses from your
Antonietta

Letter 64

November 17, 1936

Dear Jesus in the Eucharist,

I love you very, very much! Save and free many souls from Purgatory. Who knows when Christmas will come? It will be a very beautiful day. I always think about when it will come. I wish it was today. I know that there are still many days to go. I wish it would come soon.

Dear Jesus, I am very happy that you free some souls from Purgatory. I would like everyone to go to Heaven to be with you.

Dear Jesus, I will make many sacrifices so that you will make many sinners convert.

Dear Jesus, bless my parents, help my sister, heal Caterina's throat, and make the sorrowful pains pass from my grandma and aunt.

Dear Jesus, blessings and kisses from your dear,

Antonietta

P.S. Tomorrow, I will write a beautiful letter to you and Mary.

Letter 65

November 18, 1936

Dear Baby Jesus,

I love you very much! Will Christmas come soon so I can receive you in Holy Communion? It will be a beautiful day!

Dear Jesus, save many souls from Purgatory and convert many sinners.

Dear Jesus, make all evil leave from my mommy, help my daddy, my sister, my mommy, my aunt, and heal Caterina's throat.

Dear Jesus, save me from every danger, and also my parents, and everyone in the world.

Blessings and kisses from your
Antonietta

Letter 66

Dear Mary,
I love you very much!

Dear Mary, tell Jesus to give many graces to me and to everyone in the world. I would be very happy to save souls and free everyone in the world. I ask this with all my heart.

Dear Mary, I am happy to receive Jesus on my beautiful First Communion, but I would like to receive him from your hands. At least that would make me happier.

Dear Mary, tell Jesus to free many souls from Purgatory. That would also make me happy. Tell him too that I will make many sacrifices so that they go to Heaven.

Dear Mary, tell Jesus to make me grow in goodness, and to grow better always, so I can go to Heaven with Him, and also with you, dear Mary.

Dear Mary, blessings and kisses from your
Antonietta

Letter 67

November 19, 1936

Dear Jesus in the Eucharist,

I love you very much. I suffer from this illness so that many souls are saved and go to Heaven to glorify you.

Dear Jesus, tell your mommy that I also love her very much.

Dear Jesus, convert many sinners because that, at least, makes me happier.

I can't wait for Christmas to come, so I can receive you in Holy Communion.

Many blessings and kisses from your
Antonietta

Letter 68

Dear Baby Jesus,

I know that we still have thirty-three more days until Christmas, but to me it seems too many! I wish Christmas would come very soon—no, even sooner! Dear Jesus, I love you very, very much, and I will be very happy when Christmas comes.

Dear Jesus, I carry this illness so that many souls can go to Heaven and glorify you. That, at least, gives me happiness. But I wish the whole world would glorify you.

Dear Jesus, I will be very happy when you enter into my heart so that I will be able to ask you for many graces, and not only the four graces that I want to ask you for now. First, make me come to Heaven. Second, make me grow better always. Third, also make my daddy, my mommy, my sister, my grandma, my aunts and uncles come to Heaven, too. Fourth, help the whole world. Dear Jesus, I was wrong, I would like another grace, that of saving many souls.

Many blessings and kisses from your
Antonietta

Letter 69

Dear Mary of the Sacred Heart of Jesus,
I love you very much! Tell Jesus to bless all clerics and the Church.

Dear Mary, tell Jesus to bless my daddy, my mommy, my sister, and the whole world.

Kisses and blessings from your dear,
Antonietta

Letter 70

November 21, 1936

Dearest God the Father,

I am very happy that your Son is coming into my heart. I want to fill my heart with light and little flowers so that he will at least find it more beautiful.

Dear God the Father, I love you very, very—*no!*—super very much! And I am very happy that you free souls to come to Heaven to glorify you.

Dear God the Father, convert sinners by thousands upon thousands!

Dear God the Father... Father! Father! I would repeat this beautiful name forever!

Dear God the Father, make Christmas come soon. I would like to receive your Son into my heart.

Dear God the Father, help my parents, my sister, and me, and let us come to Heaven to glorify you.

Dear God the Father, tell Jesus that I am very happy to receive him and tell him also that, when I write him a letter, he will hear in all these letters that I love him.

Dear God the Father, many blessings and kisses from your dear daughter,

Antonietta

Letter 71

November 21, 1936

Dear Mary,
Blessings and kisses from your,
Antonietta

Letter 72

Dear God the Father,

God! Father! Father! What a beautiful name!

Dear God the Father, heal me soon so I can receive the Sacrament of Reconciliation next Sunday.

Dear God the Father, I adore this name because it means Father of the Whole World!

Dear God the Father, I love you very, very much!

Dear Father, bless the whole world. First, bless my parents, and my sister, and everyone else, and send them all to Heaven. Save many souls so that they come to Heaven to glorify you.

Dear God the Father, first of all, bless the Church, and the clerics, and the laity.

Dear God the Father, tell Jesus that I am very happy to receive him and I hope that he will be happy, too.

Dear God the Father, many blessings and kisses from Your daughter,

Antonietta

Letter 73

Dear God the Father,

Father, I love you very, very much!

Give me many graces and make Christmas come soon so that I can receive Jesus into my heart.

Dear God the Father, tell Jesus that my heart hopes to be very beautiful.

Dear God the Father, I know that your son, Jesus, suffered much, but tell him that I will make many sacrifices to make amends for sins.

Dear God the Father, many blessings and kisses from Your daughter,

Antonietta

Letter 74

November 25, 1936

Dear God the Father,

I love you very—*no!*—super very much!

God the Father, make Christmas come soon and I will come to receive Your Son, Jesus, into my heart!

Dear God the Father, I did not write last evening because my mommy was not here, but I am writing a beautiful letter this evening.

Dear God the Father, tell Your Son, Jesus, that I love him very much and also tell him that I wait for him a lot in my heart.

Dear God the Father, I wish that you would free the many souls in Purgatory so that they can go to Heaven to glorify you. I also wish that you would convert many sinners, especially the Abyssinians.[16]

---

[16] In the Great Schism of 1054, the Abyssinian Church was one of the groups that split from Catholicism. Throughout the second millennia, they have incorporated into their tradition elements of the Copts, Judaism, and paganism; and as a result, their faith promulgates monophysitism—the Catholic heresy that believes that Jesus has only one nature. For centuries the Abyssinian Church was a dominant religion in Ethiopia. Even though Pope Pius XI condemned Mussolini's annexation of Ethiopia through the Second Italo-Ethiopian War, Italian Catholics of the 1930s, such as Antonietta's family, were keenly aware of the need to evangelize Ethiopia's Abyssinian Church.

Dear God the Father, tell Jesus that I will make a beautiful place for him in my heart, so that in my heart, he can sleep well and rest.

Dear God the Father, I ask you for this grace, that you help my daddy.

Dear God the Father, make me grow in goodness.

Dear God the Father, many blessings and lots of kisses from your daughter,

Antonietta

Letter 75

November 25, 1936

Dear Baby Jesus,
Jesus, many blessings and hugs from your
Antonietta

Dear Mary,
Many hugs and thoughts from your daughter,
Antonietta

Letter 76

November 26, 1936

Dear Baby Jesus,

I love you and I hope that Christmas will come soon so I can receive you in Holy Communion. That night will be very beautiful! I'll come to receive you when you are born and my heart will be happy, happy, happy!

Dear Jesus, bless my parents, my sister, the Church, the clergy, my grandparents, my uncles and aunts, and everyone!

Dear Jesus, tell dear Mary that I love her very much and that I will also ask her for many graces on the day of my First Communion.

Dear Jesus, I really want you to make Christmas come soon.

Dear Jesus, I know of only three graces that I would like to ask for, so I will ask them of you now. First, make me come to Heaven. Second, make me grow in goodness. Third, help my mommy, my daddy, my sister, and everyone in the world. Dear Jesus, actually, I have another grace to ask for, that you convert many sinners, especially those in Abyssinia.

Dear Jesus, many blessings and many kisses from your dear,

Antonietta

Letter 77

November 28, 1936

Dear God the Father,

I am very happy that tomorrow I will go to Confession for the first time and that you will forgive me.

Dear God the Father, I am very happy and I thank you!

Dear God the Father, I love you very, very—*no!*—super very much! I hope Christmas will come soon so that I can receive Your Son, Jesus, into my heart and tell Jesus that I am very happy. Only twenty-six days to go, but I wish that, if it cannot come tomorrow, then it could be in five days. Dear God the Father, tell Jesus that I will ask him for many graces, and that these are the graces that I would like. First, make me go to Heaven. Second, make me grow in goodness. And third, help my parents.

Dear God the Father, many blessings and kisses from your daughter,

Antonietta

Letter 78

November 29, 1936

Dear God the Father,

I love you very, very much! I am happy that I went to Confession today, but I was also a little bad. But I promise to be better tomorrow, at school, at home with my sister, and I will especially be good for you.

Dear God the Father, what a beautiful name. It makes me so very happy! I would always repeat your beautiful name... Father of All the Earth... Father of Divinity.

Dear God the Father, I will not stain my soul anymore, and I will try to make my soul more and more beautiful to go to Heaven.

Dear God the Father, help everyone in the world, but especially my parents, my sister, and everyone in the world. Bless my teacher and everyone in the world.

Many blessings and kisses from your daughter,

Antonietta

P.S. Dear God the Father, make Christmas come soon, so that I can receive your son, Jesus.

Letter 79

December 1, 1936

Dear God the Father,

I love you very much and I hope that Christmas will come soon so I can receive Jesus. Make me be better always, so I can receive Jesus into my heart.

Dear God the Father! What a beautiful name, Father! Father of the whole world! Father of the good and the bad. What a beautiful name! I want to say it always, dear Father God.

Dear God the Father, bless my parents, my sister, and especially the pope. Bless everyone in the world!

Dear God the Father, receive many blessings and kisses from your dear daughter,

Antonietta

Letter 80

December 1, 1936[17]

Dear God the Father,

I love you very, very much, and I hope that Christmas will come soon so, at least, I can receive Your Son, Jesus, into my heart!

Dear God the Father, I love you very, very—*no!*—super very much! I know that I wrote to you already, but I want to write again.

Dear God the Father, help my parents, my sister, my grandparents, my uncles and aunts, Caterina, and everyone!

Dear God the Father, how beautiful is your name! I will repeat it always—*no!*—always and always because I like it so much.

Dear God the Father, tell Jesus that I love him very much. Tell him also that I will be very happy when he enters into my heart. And also tell him that I want many graces.

---

[17] Two of Antonietta's letters for December lack dates: This letter marked for December 1, 1936, and the letter placed on December 22, 1936. After careful discernment and prayer, and through the besought intercession of Venerable Antonietta Meo, the context clues of each letter indicate that the dates assigned to them in this manuscript are generally accurate and in keeping with the overall narrative of her writings, which unfold the story of Antonietta's holiness.

Dear God the Father, what a beautiful name! Father! Father of the whole world! Father of infinite goodness!

Dear God the Father, tell Mary that I also love her very much.

Many blessings and kisses from your daughter, Antonietta

Letter 81

December 2, 1936

Dear God the Father,

I love you very, very much! Only a few days to go until Christmas. I wonder how beautiful that day will be!

Dear God the Father, tell Jesus that I am very happy that Christmas is coming! And also tell him that I will ask him for many graces.

Dear God the Father, make me always grow better so I can be worthy to receive Your Son, Jesus.

Dear God the Father, tell Jesus that I will now tell him the graces that I want. First, make me go to Heaven. Second, save me from danger. Third, help my parents and make many souls go to heaven.

Dear God the Father, many blessings and kisses from your daughter,

Antonietta

P.S. Many kisses and blessings to Mary and Jesus.

Letter 82

December 3, 1936

Dear Jesus in the Eucharist,

I love you very much, dear Jesus. Make Christmas come soon so that I can receive you in Holy Communion.

Dear Jesus, I will always make many sacrifices so that I can come to Heaven to enjoy all its beauty, but the most important thing to see is God.

Dear Jesus, I am very happy and I long for you to enter into my heart. I will make many sacrifices because it makes you happier, and because my heart is closer to you in the Holy Tabernacle. I want to always be your lamp, not near you in person, but near you in thought. And I would love to be your little flower perfuming the Holy Tabernacle.[18]

---

[18] Antonietta's letters describe two kinds of "little flowers." Beginning in Letter 29, she indicates that she would like to make little flowers (*fioretti*), which she understood as little sacrifices, similar to those of St. Francis of Assisi. In this letter, she indicates that she would like to be a little flower (*fiorellino*), which more literally translates as floret, but her meaning is more accurately rendered as "little flower," since the word "fiorellino" most often occurs in the Italian translation of Thérèse of Lisieux's autobiography (S. Teresa Lisieux: *Storia di un'anima*) that was available in Antonietta's childhood, and would have likely been read to her by her mother, who also spent many hours teaching her the Catechism. However, St. Thérèse's "little flower" spirituality is not limited to the word "fiorellino;" the Italian manuscript

Dear Jesus, I will make many sacrifices so that you will free souls from Purgatory and bring them to Heaven to glorify God the Father.

Dear Jesus, I would like to always be your little flower.

Dear Jesus, many blessings and kisses from your dear,

Antonietta

---

also translates "little flower" as "fiore umile" or "l'umile fiore" (humble flower), which would have given Antonietta a broader understanding of St. Thérèse's little way of holiness. Thus, in desiring to be Jesus's little flower that perfumes his Holy Tabernacle, she also expresses a twin-desire to have a beautiful and humble soul through little sacrifices for him.

Letter 83

December 4, 1936

Dear Jesus in the Eucharist,

I love you very much. Make Christmas come soon so I can receive you in Holy Communion.

Dear Jesus, I want to be Your lamp that burns day and night before You.

Dear Jesus, when Christmas comes, I will ask you for many graces, dear Jesus. And I will make many little sacrifices, dear Jesus, to free many souls.

Dear Jesus, make me always grow better.

Dear Jesus, I love you very—*no!*—super very, very much! And I will do many sacrifices to save many souls so that they can go to Heaven to glorify God.

Dear Jesus, bless my parents, my sister, the Church, the clergy, my grandparents, my uncles and aunts, and my friends.

Dear Jesus, I am very happy that you are about to enter into my heart for the first time.

Many blessings and kisses from your dear,

Antonietta

Letter 84

December 5, 1936

Dear Jesus in the Eucharist,

I hope that Christmas will come soon! Dear Jesus, I love you very much! I am very, very happy about receiving you into my heart. Dear Jesus, when I am old enough, I would like to be a nun, so I can be your bride. Would you be happy with me as your bride?

Dear Jesus, bless my parents, my sister, the Church, the clergy, my grandparents, my uncles and aunts, all good and bad people, and help everyone who asks for my prayers.

Bless my grandparents and all the dead, especially my brother and sister.[19]

Dear Jesus, I will offer many sacrifices so that you will convert many sinners and free many souls from Purgatory, so that they come to Heaven to glorify you, together with the Father and the Holy Spirit, but the Father first of all.

Caresses, blessings, and kisses, from your
Antonietta

P.S. Dear Jesus, only nineteen days until I receive you into my heart!

---

[19] Antonietta is referring to her deceased brother and sister, Giovanni (1919-1921) and Carmela (1924-1926).

Letter 85

December 6, 1936

Dearest Jesus in the Eucharist,

I hope that Christmas will come soon!

I want to make many little sacrifices. They will at least make me happier because I will have prepared a more beautiful room in my heart.

Dear Jesus, I love you very much, and I will make many little sacrifices, firstly because you will give me souls to save sinners, and secondly because they will go to Heaven to glorify the Father, you, and the Holy Spirit.

Dear Jesus, bless the Church, the clergy, my parents, my sister, my relatives, my friends, good and bad people, and may your blessing save many bad people.

Dear Jesus, I will always be good and I would like to be your lamp, not near you in person but in thought. Then I will think of you forever and ever!

Blessings and many caresses and kisses, my dear Jesus.

Antonietta

Letter 86

December 7, 1936

Dear God the Father, I love you very much. Make Christmas come soon so that I can receive Your Son, Jesus.

Dear God the Father, many blessings and kisses from your dear daughter,

Antonietta

Letter 87

December 7, 1936

Dear God the Father,

I love you very much! Make Christmas come soon so that, at least, I can receive Holy Communion and tell Jesus that I love him very, very much!

Dear God the Father, I know that I already told you, but I still want to say, *I love you very much!*

Dear God the Father, when will Christmas come? I want to receive your son Jesus into my heart.

Dear God the Father, save souls so that they come to Heaven to glorify you. I am very happy that you save them. I especially pray for Spain and Abyssinia.[20]

Dear God the Father, many blessings and kisses from your dear daughter,

Antonietta

---

[20] On Abyssinia, see the footnote for Letter 74. On Spain, Antonietta wrote this letter five months after the beginning of the Spanish Civil War (17 July 1936 – 1 April 1939). Leftist groups in Spain became strongly antichurch and anticlerical. They committed numerous acts of violence, including the *Red Terror*, which refers to the indiscriminate execution of tens of thousands of Spaniards, including nearly 7,000 Catholic clerics.

Letter 88

December 7, 1936

Dear Mary,

I know that your novena[21] has begun and I will make many sacrifices and little flowers.

Blessings and kisses from your daughter,

Antonietta

---

[21] Antonietta is referring to the Novena to the Immaculate Conception, which in the Church traditionally begins on November 29th and ends on December 7th, not only in preparation during Advent for Christmas, but also in preparation for the Solemnity of the Immaculate Conception, on December 8th.

Letter 89

December 8, 1936[22]

Dear Mary,

I love you very much. Tell Jesus to forgive me because in church I wasn't still.

Dear Mary, tell Jesus that I love him very much.

Dear Mary, I am happy that today is your feast. Dear Mary, on this feast of you and Jesus, I will make many little sacrifices. Tell Jesus to let me die before I commit a mortal sin.

Dear Mary, it isn't enough that I told you once that I love you very much, but I must say again just how much I love you! You always help me with your grace. Today, I promise that I will always be good.

Dear Mary, many blessings and caresses and kisses from your daughter,

Antonietta

---

[22] This day, December 8, is the Solemnity of the Immaculate Conception: The celebration of Mary being naturally conceived by her parents, Saint Joachim and Saint Anne, without the stain of Original Sin. The celebration occurs nine months before the Feast of the Birth of Mary, on September 8.

Letter 90

December 9, 1936

Dear Baby Jesus,

Firstly, about that sinner, make him better.[23]

Dear Jesus, for love of you, I love everyone, the good and the bad, and I give them all to you.

Dear Jesus, I love you very much, and I hope that this blessed Christmas will come soon, so that I can at least receive you in Holy Communion.

Dear Jesus, save me from all dangers. Dear Jesus, I want to be very good to save many souls and send them to Heaven, especially that man I just mentioned, but want to mention again.

Dear Jesus, tell God the Father that I love him very much. I will do many small sacrifices to make amends for my sins and for the many, many ugly sins of others.

Dear Jesus, I send you many caresses, blessings, and kisses, from your dear,

Antonietta

Dear Mary, I send you many blessings and kisses from your,

Antonietta

---

[23] The identity of the sinful man remains a mystery. He might be the same person whom Antonietta prays for in other letters, or he might be a stranger among many for whom she intercedes. For more details, read the footnote in Letter 44.

Letter 91

December 9, 1936

Dear Baby Jesus,

I love you very—*no!*—super very, very much!

I repent and ask pardon with all my heart for the tantrum I threw. Tomorrow, I will make many sacrifices to make amends.

Dear Jesus, I would like to be a nun. Does that make you happy?

Letter 92

Dear Jesus,

I had to stop writing yesterday, but I am continuing tonight.

Dear Jesus, I want to be a nun. Does that make you happy, dear Jesus?

I cannot wait for Christmas to come, dear Jesus, to receive you into my heart and ask you for many graces. Now, I ask you for three, but at Christmas I will ask you for many. First, make me go to Heaven. Second, make me grow in goodness. Third, help my parents and bring them to Heaven.

Dear Jesus, tell God the Father that I love him very much, and tell him also that I will make many little sacrifices so that I will be happier when I receive you into my heart. Today, I made a few sacrifices, but tomorrow I will make many. Help me to do so because I cannot do it alone.

Blessings and kisses from your dear,
Antonietta

Letter 93

December 11, 1936

Dear Baby Jesus,

I love you very much and I am very happy that Christmas is coming so that I can receive you into my heart. I will make many little flowers to prepare a beautiful room for you in my heart, dear Jesus.

Dear Jesus, bless us, and receive many blessings and kisses from your dear,

Antonietta

Letter 94

December 12, 1936

Dear Jesus in the Eucharist,

I love you very much. Dear Jesus, make Christmas come soon so that I can receive you in Holy Communion.

Dear Jesus, I want everyone to go to Heaven to glorify the Most Holy Trinity.

Dear Jesus, tell Mary that I love her very much.

Dear Jesus, above all, bless the Holy Father, who represents you. Bless the Church and the clergy, dear Jesus, then bless my family, then my relatives, my friends, and the whole world.

Blessings and many kisses to dear Mary.

And caresses and many blessings to you from your dear,

Antonietta

Letter 95

December 13, 1936

Dear Great Jesus,

Dear Jesus in the Eucharist,

I love you very, very much! Ten more days![24] What joy! I will receive you into my heart with great love!

Dear Jesus, tell God the Father that I love him very much.

Dear Jesus, I thank you that there are only ten more days. I will be so happy when I receive you.

Dear Jesus, I want to be a nun and I want to be very good, dear Jesus, and I will make many little sacrifices to save many souls, dear Jesus. Are you happy that I will be a nun?

Dear Jesus, bless the Pope and everyone. Dear Jesus, tell Mary that I will write to her tomorrow, and that I love her very much.

Many blessings and kisses from your

Antonietta

---

[24] Antonietta has been writing that she will receive Jesus on Christmas, but in this letter, which was written in the evening, she writes that she will receive him in ten days, on December 24, the Christmas Vigil.

Letter 96

December 14, 1936

Dear Jesus in the Eucharist,[25]

Only nine more days to go! How beautiful! How happy I will be when I receive you for the first time in my heart. Dear Jesus, I love you very, very, very much, dear Jesus! Tell God the Father that I love him very much.

Dear Jesus, thank you so much that Christmas will be coming soon.

Dear Jesus, bless the Holy Father, the Church, my parents, my sister, my grandparents, and my friends.

Dear Jesus, many blessings and kisses from your dear,

Antonietta

---

[25] Although Antonietta wrote in her previous letter, December 13, 1936, that she would write a letter to Mary on the following day, December 14, no letter is evident. If a letter was written, it has been lost.

Letter 97

December 15, 1936

Dear Jesus in the Eucharist,

I am happy that in a few days it will be Christmas, so that I can receive you in Holy Communion within my heart, dear Jesus. I wonder how beautiful that day will be! I love you very much and I wish to save souls so that they go to Heaven to glorify the Most Holy Trinity, but especially the Father.

Dear Jesus, I will be very happy when that holy day comes, so that I can receive you in Holy Communion. I am not thinking about my dress, instead I'm thinking about the dress of my soul. I want it to be beautiful and immaculately white.

Dear Jesus, tell Mary that I love her very much.

Dear Jesus, help that priest. And I entrust that sick woman to you. Strengthen her to endure her pain.[26]

Dear Jesus, I thank you that I am six years old today.

---

[26] The identities of the priest and the sick woman whom Antonietta mentions remain a mystery. However, because Antonietta had to return to S. Stefano Rotondo's Clinic to receive injections of calcium, which were very painful, it is likely that she is referring to a chaplain administering to a patient the Sacrament of the Anointing of the Sick, or the Viaticum, or both.

Dear Jesus, receive many caresses and kisses and blessings from your dear,
Antonietta

Letter 98

December 16, 1936

Dear Baby Jesus

I love you very much and I hope that Christmas comes soon so that I can receive you into my heart. I will prepare for you a beautiful, little, very soft cradle, so you can sleep well, dear Jesus.

Then I will make little sacrifices: first, for the conversion of all sinners; second, to free the souls in Purgatory so that they can go to Heaven to glorify the Most Holy Trinity; and third, to help me, my mommy, my daddy, my sister, and everyone!

Dear Jesus, I will be very happy when you enter into my heart for the first time.

Dear Jesus, tell God the Father that I thank him, thank you, and the Holy Spirit, too, that Christmas will be coming soon.

Bless my parents, the Church, the Pope, and the whole world.

Blessings and caresses and kisses from Your dear,
Antonietta

Letter 98

December 17, 1936

Dear Jesus in the Eucharist,

I love you very, very—*no!*—super very much, dear Jesus. I am very happy that it will be Christmas in less than seven days, and that I can receive you in Holy Communion.

Dear Jesus, free many souls from Purgatory so that they can go to Heaven to glorify the Most Holy Trinity.

Dear Jesus, tell God the Father that I am happy that he inspired me to make my first Communion on Christmas day, because it is the very same day that Jesus was born in the world to save us and to die on the Cross. Dear Jesus, tell God the Father that I love him very much and that I thank him that Christmas will be coming soon.

Dear Jesus, bless the Church, the Pope, and the clergy. Dear Jesus, give a lot of strength to that sick woman so that she can endure her sorrowful pains. I also give to you that priest. And especially help that sinner. Dear Jesus, bless my parents, me, my sister, my uncles, my aunt, my grandpas and grandmas, and everyone in the world. And I especially entrust to you the conversion of many sinners.

Dear Jesus, I want Mary to give me her son with her hands.

Blessings, caresses, and kisses from your dear,
Antonietta

Letter 100

December 18, 1936

Dear Baby Jesus,

I love you very much. What joy for me that there are six more days until I receive you in Holy Communion!

Dear Jesus, tell God the Father that I love him very much. Dear Jesus, also tell God the Father that I thank him and you, because in a few days it will be Christmas!

Dear Jesus, bless the Church, the Pope, and the clergy.

Dear Jesus, save many souls from Purgatory so that they come to Heaven to glorify the Most holy Trinity, and especially God the Father.

Dear Jesus, tell Mary that I wish to receive you from her hands.

Dear Jesus, bless my parents, my sister, and everyone in the world. Dear Jesus, make yourself known and loved by many souls, especially to those in Abyssinia, and to many others who do not know you.

Dear Jesus, tell Mary that I love her very much.

Dear Jesus, many blessings and caresses and kisses from your dear,

Antonietta

Letter 101

December 19, 1936

Dear Jesus in the Eucharist,

I love you very much and I hope that Christmas will come soon so that I can receive you in Holy Communion. Free many souls from Purgatory so that they can go to Heaven to glorify the Holy Trinity and especially the Father.

Dear Jesus, I am so happy that we only have four days to go!

Dear Jesus, tell God the Father that I love him very much.

Dear Jesus, I got a red mark in school today. Forgive this sin.

Dear Jesus, it is not enough that I said it only one time, but I say again that I love you very much! Also, heal mommy.

Dear Jesus, bless the pope, the church, the clergy, my parents, my sister, Caterina, and everyone in the world!

Many blessings and kisses from your
Antonietta

Dear Mary, many blessings and kisses from your
Antonietta

Letter 102

December 20, 1936

Dear Baby Jesus,

I love you very, very, very much! And I am really happy that Christmas will come soon so that I can receive you in Holy Communion.

Dear Jesus, I want to do lots and lots of little flowers for the salvation of many souls.

Dear Jesus, tell God the Father that I love him very much. Dear Jesus, also thank him and the Holy Spirit because there are only three days left until Christmas! Dear Jesus, I am very happy that in a few days you will come into my heart, dear Jesus! It is not enough to say it only once, but I must say again that I love you very much, dear Jesus!

Dear Jesus, bless the Church, the Pope, the clergy, then my parents, my sister, and everyone in the world.

Dear Jesus, convert many sinners, especially those who do not know you.

You know, dear Jesus, that I also love black people,[27] those who do not know you, and bad people

---

[27] The text states, "io voglio bene anche ai neri," literally translated as "I also love the blacks," a common way for a child of 1936-Italy to refer to dark skinned people; and in fact, the descriptor can still be found in the modern Italian writings of Paola Tabet's *La pelle giusta* (2016) and Oriana Fallaci's *Le radici dell'odio* (2017). This translation clarifies Antonietta's meaning by rendering her phrase as "black

who do not love you, because they are all souls, dear Jesus.

Dear Jesus, many blessings, caresses, and kisses form your dear

Antonietta Jesus

---

people." However, because she does not use this descriptor in any other letter, and because it appears so incongruous with the vast majority of her supplications to Jesus, it is reasonable to conclude that she is referring to the dark skinned people of the Abyssinian church, which is in modern day Ethiopia, Africa, and which would be consistent with her desire for their conversion, as seen in Letters 74, 76, 87, 100, 105, and109.

Letter 103

December 20, 1936

Dear Daddy,

I love you very much and I will always pray to Jesus for you, dear daddy, for Jesus to help you. Pray for me, too, because Jesus always makes me be better.

Dear Daddy, I will obey you forever, I will always be good to make you happy, and I will try to never sin.

Dear Daddy, I will be very happy on Christmas day because then I will receive my Jesus into my heart.

Dear Daddy, blessings and kisses from your dear daughter,

Antonietta

Letter 104

December 21, 1936

Dear Great Jesus,

I love you very much.

Dear Jesus, I am very happy that, in two days, it will be Christmas.

Dear Jesus, I want to be a nun so that, at least, I can be your spouse.

Dear Jesus, I want to save many souls.

Dear Jesus, I want to be very good. Help me to do so because I cannot do anything alone. Dear Jesus, I want to be a saint. Help me to make many little sacrifices, and to grow better always.

Dear Jesus, tell God the Father that I love him very much, and that I thank the Most Holy Trinity that it will soon be Christmas.

Dear Jesus, let me tell you all the graces that I have been asking for. First, make me come to Heaven. Second, save many souls. Third, convert many sinners. Fourth, make my parents and my sister come to Heaven.

Blessings, caresses, and kisses from your dear, Antonietta

P.S. Dear Jesus, tell God the Father that I told him once, but that I must say again that I love him very, very much!

Letter 105

December 22, 1936[28]

Dear Jesus in the Eucharist,

Today I made two little flowers. Truthfully, they were too few. But tomorrow I will make more and I will be good.

Dear Jesus, make Christmas come soon so I can receive you in Holy Communion, and I will be good to make you happier.

Dear Jesus, I love you very much. Help the Abyssinians to know and love you. I also entrust to you that person whom you know.

Dear Jesus, protect my teacher, me, my sister, my parents, and also Sister Bartolina. I love them all so much!

Blessings and kisses,
Antonietta

---

[28] Two of Venerable Antonietta Meo's letters for December lack dates: This letter marked for December 22, 1936; and the other placed as the second letter of December 1, 1936. For more information, read the footnote in Letter 80.

Letter 106

December 23, 1936

Dearest Jesus in the Eucharist,

Thank you for healing me. Only you know, dear Jesus, only you know how happy I am! Just one more day and then I will receive you into my heart, dear Jesus!

Dear Jesus, I will ask for many graces then, but let me tell you everything now—that I will love you, that I will thank you, and that I will ask you only for necessary things. First, bring my parents and my sister to Heaven with you. Second, save many souls, convert many sinners, and free many souls from Purgatory. Third, help everyone who has asked for my prayers. Fourth, dear Jesus, heal me so that I can walk better. Fifth, heal my parents, bless the Church, the Pope, the clergy, my parents, my sister, my friends, and everyone in the world.

Love, caresses, and kisses, dear Jesus. I cannot wait to receive you into my heart so that I can love you more!

Love,
Antonietta and Jesus[29]

---

[29] Since Antonietta was just learning how to write at this time, she dictated this letter to her mother before signing it by her own hand: "Antonietta and Jesus." In later letters, beginning in Letter 127, she signs several "Antonietta of Jesus," as if she had already become a nun and taken a

I love you very much!

religious name, similar to Saint Thérèse of Lisieux, called Saint Thérèse of the Child Jesus and the Holy Face. Antonietta alternates between these three kinds of signatures: Thirty-five letters are signed "Antonietta e Gesù" (Antonietta and Jesus), seven are signed "Antonietta di Gesù" (Antonietta of Jesus), and two are signed "Antonietta Gesù" (Antonietta Jesus). Antonietta's preferred signature— "Antonietta and Jesus"—reveals the innocence of her childhood and how she viewed her relationship with Jesus. On the one hand, her letters reveal her awareness of his human nature through his suffering and his divine nature in the Eucharist; yet on the other hand, her behavior toward Jesus evokes the kind of playfulness 5-year-olds develop in the psychological stage of Cooperative Play, when children form meaningful friendships through intimate interaction. Such is the case in Letter 24 where she writes: "Dear Baby Jesus, come to school with me and bless everyone." Similarly, Dino De Carolis's *Antonietta Meo. La sapienza dei piccoli del Vangelo* (2004) also notes how Antonietta was overheard whispering to her church's tabernacle, "Jesus, come and play with me!" Antonietta's dictation to her mother reveals the depth of her soul while her own hand exposes the breadth of her child's heart.

Letter 107

December 24, 1936, 9 P.M.

Dear Jesus in the Eucharist,

I am very happy that in a few hours I will receive you in the Holy Eucharist, dear Jesus.

Dear Jesus, tell God the Father and the Holy Spirit "Thank you" because in a few hours I will receive the beautiful Holy Eucharist, then I will be very, very joyful!

Dear Jesus, I adore you very, very, very much!

Dear Jesus, tell Mary that I want to receive you from her hands.

Dear Jesus, help the Church, the Pope, the clergy, my parents, and everyone in the world.

Come! Come, O My Jesus!

From your

Antonietta and Jesus

Letter 108

December 25, 1936

I love mommy and daddy very much!
Antonietta

Letter 109

December 26, 1936

Dear Jesus in the Eucharist,

I love you very much and I ask you for those graces that I asked for in Communion, and for those that I have not asked for. I promise that I want to always be good, but help me, because without you I can do nothing.

Dear Jesus, tell God the Father that I thank him, you, and the Holy Spirit for Christmas.

Dear Jesus, also tell God the Father that I thank him because you came into my heart.

Dear Jesus, tell Mary that I love her very, very— *no!*—super very much!

Dear Jesus, I want you to save many souls, and convert many sinners, especially those in Abyssinia, those who do not know you, and their priests who do know you.

Dear Jesus, many blessings and kisses and caresses from your

Antonietta and Jesus

Letter 110

December 30, 1936

Dear Jesus in the Eucharist,
I love you very, very much!

Dear Jesus, when you return again into my heart in the Holy Eucharist, place your grace into the wardrobe of my soul, which is made of sacrifices, and leave it there until you come for the last time into my heart. And then, when I am dead, your grace will fly my soul to Heaven, where I will see you, your Father, the Holy Spirit, and dear Mary, and where I will be happy with you all.

Dear Jesus (I love you, dear Jesus), I will come to ask and receive many graces.

Dear Jesus, blessings and kisses from your dear,
Antonietta and Jesus

Letter 111

December 30, 1936

Good daddy, you are loving.

A kiss to you and a blessing to your heart.

Loving daddy, I will pray to Mary that she will always make you as healthy as you are now, and even better.

Dear daddy, say a little prayer for me, that Jesus makes me good, that Jesus makes me walk well, and that Jesus makes you happy.

Many best wishes from your

Nennolina

Letter 112

January 1, 1937

Dear Jesus in the Eucharist,

I promise that this year, beginning today, I will be better than last year. Help me to be good because without your help I can do nothing.

Dear Jesus, I love you very much! And I pray that you please bless the Church, heal the Pope,[30] bless the clergy, my parents, my family, my friends, and the whole world, and also heal Father Orlando.

Dear Jesus, tell God the Father that I love him very much and that I also promise to be good. And tell him to give me many souls, so that they go to Heaven to glorify the Most Holy Trinity.

Dear Jesus, thank you for coming into my heart, and forgive me if I was not good.

Dear Jesus, many blessings, caresses, and kisses from your dear,

Antonietta Jesus

---

[30] Pope Pius XI had grown very ill by this time, which he briefly refers to in his remarkable encyclical *Mit Brennender Sorge* (March 19, 1937). Antonietta will repeatedly pray for the Pope's health until her own death.

Letter 113

January 3, 1937

Dear Jesus in the Eucharist,

I love you very much.

Dear Jesus, free many souls from Purgatory.

Dear Jesus, forgive all the sins I have done today.

Dear Jesus, I want to spend all day on Calvary, under your cross, near Mary.

Dear Jesus, I ask again for you to forgive all my sins.

Dear Jesus, I cannot come to receive you in Holy Communion, but I wish that you would come at least spiritually into my heart every morning.[31]

Dear Jesus, many blessings and caresses and kisses from your dear Antonietta.

Antonietta and Jesus

---

[31] This date, January 3, 1937, was on a Sunday. No sufficient documentation explains why Antonietta could not attend mass. However, because she would die exactly six months from this date (July 3, 1937), her absence is likely to have been a result of her metastasizing cancer. She will write one more letter tomorrow, January 4, but the next will come five days later, on January 9, where she will write about offering all her suffering to God, indicating that her painful ordeal likely prevented her from writing.

Letter 114

January 4, 1937

Dear Jesus in the Eucharist,

I love you very much.

Dear Jesus, I want to be your spouse.

Dear Jesus, thank the Most Holy Trinity that I could receive you into my heart.

Dear Jesus, I wish to save many souls so they go to Heaven to glorify the Most Holy Trinity.

Dear Jesus, when I first enter church, I want to be still. I want to be still always.

Dear Jesus, tell God the Father that I love him very much.

Dear Jesus, bless the Church, the Holy Father, the clergy, my family, and especially my parents and me, and everyone in the world.

Dear Jesus, many blessings, caresses, and kisses from your Antonietta.

Divine Host, O Sacred Love,

Divine Host, You are honor.

Antonietta and Jesus

Letter 115

January 9, 1937

Dearest God the Father,

I wish to save many souls, and dear God the Father, I greatly wish that they go to Heaven with you.

Dear God the Father, all the sorrowful pains that I suffer, I suffer them all for you, and I will make all my actions do the same.

Dear God the Father, I wish to be a nun. Would that make you happy, dear Father God?

Dear God the Father, I love you very much. Dear God the Father, tell Jesus that I love him very much too. Dear God the Father, tell Mary that I also love her very much.

Dear God the Father, bless the Church, the Pope, the clergy, my parents, my sister, and everyone in the world.

Caresses and kisses from your
Antonietta

Letter 116

January 10, 1937

Dear Holy Spirit,

Sanctify our souls, dear Holy Spirit. Thank you for helping me find a good and holy confessor. I hope to meet him soon, dear Holy Spirit.

Dear Holy Spirit, I thank you that I had my First Communion on Christmas night.

Dear Holy Spirit, illuminate my soul so that I will be the little lamp that forever illuminates the Holy Tabernacle.

Dear Holy Spirit, bless the Pope, the Church, and the clergy first. Then bless my daddy, my mommy, my sister, and bless me, my family, and everyone in the world.

Dear Holy Spirit, I love you very, very much. Tell Jesus that I also love him very much and that I thank him for entering into my heart this morning.

Dear Holy Spirit, I send you love and many kisses. Antonietta and Jesus

Jesus from Heaven, come into my heart,
O You, who are love.

January 12, 1937

Dear Baby Jesus,

Thank you for giving me a good report card.

Dear Baby Jesus, I want to obey you always because you are almighty, and I love you very much!

Dear Baby Jesus, save many souls so that they can go to Heaven to glorify the Most Holy Trinity.

Dear Baby Jesus, I say again that I love you very much. Dear Baby Jesus, I want to always be your lamp, not only the lamp of your love, but I also want to be the lamp of your sacrifices.

Dear Baby Jesus, thank you so much for giving me the grace to receive you on Christmas night when I made my First Communion.

Dear Baby Jesus, you see how greatly my sacrifices cost me, yet I want to do many more.

Dear Baby Jesus, bless the Church, and the Holy Father and heal him soon. Bless the clergy, my family, me, and everyone in the whole world.

Dear Baby Jesus, many blessings, caresses, and kisses from your dear Antonietta.

Antonietta and Jesus

Letter 118

Dearest Holy Trinity,

Holy Trinity, I love you very, very, very much!

Dear God the Father! What a beautiful name, Father! Father of Infinite Divinity! Father, Creator of the World! Father, what a beautiful name! I want to say it over and over again! Father, what a beautiful name!

Dear Jesus, I love you very much. Dear Jesus, how much suffering you bore on the Cross! Dear Jesus, you died to save everyone. You see how bad we are, dear Jesus. I want to make many little sacrifices to make amends for the sins against you.

Dear Jesus, free many souls from Purgatory.

Dear Holy Spirit, I love you very much. Dear Holy Spirit, illuminate my soul and sanctify my body.

Dear Mary, Hail O Mary!

Holy Trinity, love and many kisses from your dear Antonietta.

Antonietta and Jesus

Letter 119

Dear Jesus Crucified,

I know that you suffered so much on the Cross and I promise to do many sacrifices to make amends for the sins that have given you so much suffering.

Dear Jesus on the Cross, I love you very—*no!*—super very much! Tell God the Father that I love him very much, too.

Dear Jesus on the Cross and dear God the Father, I love you very much, and I also love the Holy Spirit very much.

Bless, dear Jesus on the Cross, the Church, the Holy Father, the clergy, my parents, my sister, and everyone in the world.

Jesus Crucified, receive many kisses and caresses from your

Antonietta

Letter 120

January 21, 1937

Dearest God the Father,

I love you very, very, very much! Very, very—*no!*—super very much!

Dear God the Father, tell Jesus that I love him very much.

Dear God the Father, tomorrow, I want to always be under the Cross on Calvary. Today, I was there too, but I was not very good.[32] You who are so very good, forgive me.

Dear God the Father, tell the Immaculate Virgin Mary that I love her very much. Tell her to put me under her mantle, to give me many graces, and to bless me.

Dear God the Father, heal my cough.

Dear God the Father, tell Jesus that I want to do

---

[32] Antonietta writes that she stood under the Cross on Calvary today, and that she desires to stand under it tomorrow. January 21, 1937, was a Thursday, but it was also the memorial of St. Agnus, to whom Antonietta will write her next letter (Letter 121), and who is also a likely reason Antonietta meditated so profoundly on Christ's crucifixion. Although the following day, January 22, 1937, was the 2nd Friday in Ordinary Time, Fridays are considered to be days of penance, according to the Code of Canon Law: Canons 1250 - 1251. Antonietta desires to make the 2nd Friday in Ordinary Time more Lenten.

many little flowers, but without his help, I can do nothing.

Dear God the Father, tell the Holy Spirit that I love him very much and to free me from dangers.

Dear God the Father, bless everyone.

Your little daughter sends you many kisses and blessings.

Antonietta

Letter 121

January 21, 1937

Dear Saint Agnes,

I went to your feast, but I did it from my bed. I love you very much, and I want you to be my protectress, along with St. Thérèse.[33]

I love you both very much!

---

[33] In this letter, Antonietta only wrote "S. Teresa," not directly indicating Saint Thérèse of Lisieux, and unlike Letters 20 and 57 where she wrote to "S. Teresina," which is an Italian nickname for S. Teresa di Lisieux. However, because of Antonietta's devotion to the Little Flower, as indicated in the footnote in Letters 20 and 57, it is most likely that she is coupling her devotion to Saint Thérèse of Lisieux with a new devotion to Saint Agnes.

Letter 122

January 22, 1937

Dear Baby Jesus,

Dear Baby Jesus, I stood under your cross today and I had beautiful thoughts. Let me tell you about them now. Jesus, you suffered much to regain Heaven for us. I want to repay you by making many sacrifices.

Dear Mary, you saw the great suffering of your son, Jesus. I want to console you a little by making many little sacrifices.

Many kisses and blessings,
Antonietta

Letter 123

Dear Jesus on the Cross and Dear Baby Jesus,

O Jesus! You are very, very good and you see that we commit many sins. Forgive us. And let us be with you one day in Heaven.

O Jesus! You suffered so much for us, but I want to make amends for these many sins against you.

O Jesus! You were born in a cave in Bethlehem and you suffered so much on that manger straw. I want to do every possible thing to make amends for that great pain. You were so cold, and only an ox and a donkey did everything possible to keep you warm.

Dear Jesus, you came down from the stars to the world to save us and regain Heaven for us. You suffered so much pain. I want to do every possible thing to make amends for that great pain.

Dear Jesus, many blessings, caresses, and kisses from your dear Antonietta.

Antonietta and Jesus

Letter 124

January 24, 1937

Dear Daddy,

The most sweet-smelling rose of this family writes to you. It's Antonietta! And I love you very much.

Dear Daddy, I will pray so much that you will go to Heaven where you can pray for me. We love each other so much!

Dear Daddy, this rose that writes to you wants to be very good to make you happy.

Dear Daddy, I promise that I will not be cranky and that I will always be obedient.

Dear Daddy, this rose wants to suffer much for Jesus! Dear Daddy, this rose loves you so very, very much that your soul will smell very sweet.

Dear Daddy, this rose blesses you so much and sends you many kisses.

Antonietta

Letter 125

January 28, 1937

Dear Jesus Crucified,

Dear Jesus, free many souls from Purgatory so that they go to Heaven to glorify the Most Holy Trinity.

Dear Jesus, I really love you very, very, very much!

Dear Jesus, truthfully, I was not very good today. Forgive me. Tomorrow, I promise I will be good always!

Dear Jesus, I wish to become a nun. Does that make you happy?

Dear Jesus, tell God the Father that I really love him very, very much!

Dear Jesus, I wish to be holy. Help me to do many little flowers.

Dear Jesus, I want to convert many sinners so that, when they die, they can be with you in Heaven.

Dear Jesus, bless the Church, the Holy Father, the clergy, my family, and everyone in the world.

Dear Jesus, heal my mommy. Make her illness nothing.

Dear Jesus, tell the Holy Spirit to illuminate my heart with love and to bless me.

Dear Jesus, tell Mary that I love her very much, and to protect me by putting me under her mantle.

Dear Jesus, you suffered so much on the Cross. I want to do many little flowers and I want to always stay on Calvary, very near you and your mommy.

Receive many blessings, caresses, and kisses from your dear,

   Antonietta and Jesus

Letter 126

January 29, 1937

Dearest Most Holy Trinity,

Dearest God the Father, I know you love me and I love you very much too. Dear God the Father, heal my mommy.

Dearest God the Father, you who are so almighty, give me the grace to heal soon and to walk better. Dear God the Father, you who are so good, forgive me and let me soon go to receive your son, Jesus.

Dear Jesus, I love you very, very much. Dear Jesus, when you were born in a Bethlehem cave, you suffered so much and were very cold. Dear Jesus, I want to make amends for all these sorrowful pains.

Dear Holy Spirit, you are the love of the Father and the Son. Illuminate my heart and my soul and bless me.

Dear Holy Spirit, I love you very, very much. Dear Holy Spirit, when I make my Confirmation, give me all seven of your gifts.[34]

Dear Holy Spirit, many blessings, kisses, and

---

[34] As noted in *Antonietta's Story: The Beginning*, Antonietta was too young to receive the Sacrament of Confirmation, yet once a child received the Sacrament of the Eucharist, receiving the Sacrament of Confirmation shortly thereafter was an acceptable practice. However, it is likely that Antonietta was allowed to receive Confirmation so early because the illness of her metastasizing cancer was becoming evident.

caresses from your
Antonietta

Dear Mary, I love you very much. Be near me when I receive the Sacrament of Confirmation.
Antonietta and Jesus

Letter 127

January 30, 1937

Dear Jesus Crucified,

Heal my mommy. Dear Jesus, I adore you and I want to be your lily and your lamp.

Dear Jesus, I want to stay always with you on Calvary. Dear Jesus, I kiss your wounds and your feet.

Many blessings and kisses,

Antonietta of Jesus[35]

---

[35] This is the first time Antonietta changes her signature from "Antonietta and Jesus" to "Antonietta of Jesus."

Letter 128

January 31, 1937

Dear Jesus in the Eucharist,

I love you very, very much! Dear Jesus, I know you suffered so much when you were small. I want to always go to Sunday Mass, where your sacrifice on the Cross is renewed, and where you make an even greater sacrifice by locking yourself in the Most Holy Sacrament on the altar. Dear Jesus, I will come to receive you every Sunday. I would like to receive you every day, but mommy does not take me.

Dear Jesus, tell God the Father that I love him very, very much!

Dear Jesus, free many souls from Purgatory so that they come to Heaven to glorify the Most Holy Trinity.

Dear Jesus, I want to say again that I love you very, very much and that I want to be good always.

Dear Jesus, truthfully, today I was not very good, but tomorrow I promise that I will be much better.

Dear Jesus, tell God the Father that I thank him for healing mommy. I also thank you and the Holy Spirit.

Dear Jesus, I want to save many sinners, and I entrust to you especially that one sinner whom you know, and that very old sinner, and also dear Jesus, that one sinner in Saint John's Hospital.

Dear Jesus, help Russia to know you soon and make yourself known to all other bad nations.[36]

I love you, I adore you, O Jesus! And I want to always stay on Calvary under your cross.

Antonietta and Jesus

---

[36] Previous footnotes have indicated that Antonietta's family were typical Catholic conservatives during Mussolini's fascist Italy. However, despite the *Treaty on Friendship, Non-Aggression and Neutrality* that was signed by Mussolini and Stalin in 1933, ratifying Italy's recognition of the Soviet Union, Antonietta's prayer for Russia indicates that her family probably had a devotion to Our Lady of Fatima, whose 1929 message adjured believers to pray for the consecration of Russia to her Immaculate Heart. Her family's devotion to Our Lady of Fatima becomes more probable when taking into consideration Letter 134, where Antonietta might be referring to the Feast of Our Lady of Fatima, ten days after this letter was written. It is possible that Antonietta is praying for Russia in this letter because she and her family might be beginning a novena to Our Lady of Fatima on the following day, February 1.

Letter 129

February 1, 1937

Dear Jesus Crucified,

I want to save many souls so that they are saved and go to Heaven with you.

Dear Jesus, tell God the Father that I love him very, very much!

Dear Jesus, convert many sinners, especially that one sinner.

Dear Jesus, I entrust to you that one person whom you know and I ask that you grant what they desire.

Dear Jesus, I want to always be your lamp burning day and night in front of your altar.

Dear Jesus, I want to make many, many sacrifices.

Dear Holy Spirit, thank you also for healing my mommy. Make me always grow better. And bring me and my family to Heaven.

Dear Jesus, many blessings and kisses from your Antonietta.

Dear Mary, I love you very much. Your dear daughter sends you many blessings.

Antonietta and Jesus

Letter 130

February 2, 1937

Dear Mary,

Dear Mary, you are the mommy of Heaven, of Hell, and of all people. I could not celebrate the feast today because I did not go to church, but I prayed a lot. Dear Mary, I love you very, very much. Dear Mary, I know that today is your feast, and I will always pray like I did today.[37]

Dear Mary, today for your feast, make many souls in Purgatory go to Heaven and convert many sinners. I especially entrust to you that sinner whom you know. Make all sinners go to confession.

Dear Mary, I promise to always be good. I really promise!

Dear Mary, tell God the Father that I love him very much, and tell Jesus to heal my mommy soon, and tell the Holy Spirit to sanctify and illuminate me. Help me also, dear Mary.

Dear Mary, thank you also for the three graces that you and Jesus together gave me for my mommy. First, her illness became nothing. Second, she felt no pain. Third, she did not stay long in the clinic.

Dear Mary, I want to suffer with your Jesus.

---

[37] This day, February 2, was a Tuesday in 1937, and not a specific Marian celebration. However, in the Roman

From your little daughter, Antonietta.
Antonietta and Jesus

Calendar, February 2 is the Feast of Candlemas, also called
The Presentation of the Lord.

Letter 131

February 3, 1937

Dear Most Holy Trinity,

Dear God the Father, I love you very, very much.

Dear God the Father, I did not obey right away today, but you are so good and I hope you will forgive me. Dear God the Father, forgive many souls. Dear God the Father, I promise that I will be much better another day. Dear God the Father, I want to always grow better.

Dear Jesus, I love you very much, and I want to be under your cross every day. Forgive me if I have done something wrong.[38]

---

[38] No reason is given for the abrupt ending of this letter. Since it is addressed to the Trinity, it is likely that she might have intended to add a line or two to the Holy Spirit. An incomplete letter could have been a result of Antonietta's illness, which steadily increases for the next few months until her death. However, the intent of this letter to the Trinity is carried over into her next letter, tomorrow, February 4, 1937.

Letter 132

Dear Most Holy Trinity,

Dear God the Father, I love you very, very much!
Dear God the Father, what a beautiful name, Father! I
do not always say your name with much respect, but I
want to say it much more respectfully. Dear God the
Father, I ask you to forgive all the sins that I have done.
Dear God the Father, I want to do many sacrifices to
make amends for all the sins committed nowadays.
Dear God the Father, forgive many more sinners, and
make them repent, so that they come to Heaven to
glorify the Most Holy Trinity.

Dear Jesus, if I cannot come to receive you
sacramentally every day in my heart, come to me
spiritually, at least.

Dear Jesus, now that you are in my heart, remain
with me forever and ever, so that I can go to Heaven.

Dear Jesus, I want to be on Calvary always and
forever under your Cross, and I also want to be your
lamp that burns day and night in front of your Most
Holy Sacrament on the altar. Dear Jesus, I love you
very, very much!

Dear Holy Spirit, you are the love that unites the
Father and the Son. Sanctify my body and soul, and
make me come to Heaven soon. Dear Holy Spirit, you
are the Spirit of Love that inflames my heart with love
for Jesus.

Dear Holy Spirit, I love you very, very much. Dear Holy Spirit, make me always grow better, and make me go to Heaven one day.

Dear Most Holy Trinity, bless the Church, the Pope, the clergy, my family, and everyone in the whole world.

Blessings and kisses from your dear,

Antonietta and Jesus

Letter 133

February 6, 1937

Dearest Most Holy Trinity,

Dear God the Father, I love you very, very—*no!*—super very much!

Dear God the Father, save many souls.

Dear God the Father, heal mommy very soon and I promise to be better always, but you must help me and make me always be better.

Dear God the Father, mommy told me that people will gather tomorrow to say that they want to live without God, and that God's name is bad.[39] Convert them and send them your grace.

---

[39] Antonietta is likely referring to the nearly 40,000 far-left French protesters who gathered in Paris to observe the third anniversary of the *6 February 1934 crisis*, when their political opposite, France's far-right movement Action Française (composed mostly of ultra-conservative French Catholic groups), held an anti-parliamentarist counter-demonstration. Although Action Française was ideally monarchist, anti-democratic, and counter-French Revolution, they took many of their ideals from Mussolini's National Fascist Party in Italy, which was also Catholic, and of which Antonietta and her family were members. From the Italian Fascist perspective—from Antonietta's family's perspective—the 40,000 ultra-liberal French protesters in Paris on February 7, 1937, were not only anti-Action Française and anti-fascist, but many also held anti-Catholic and even atheistic sentiments.

Dear Jesus, tomorrow I will have Holy Communion in reparation for all these sinners and for all people who want to live without God.

Dear Jesus, I love you very, very much.

Dear Holy Spirit, bless me and illuminate my body and my soul, and make me always grow better.

Dear Holy Spirit, I love you very much!

Dear Most Holy Trinity, I pray that you make me always grow better.

Dearest Holy Trinity, I bless you, I adore you, and I send you many kisses.

Your Antonietta and Jesus

Letter 134

February 10, 1937

Dear Jesus in the Eucharist,

I love you very much and I am very happy that tomorrow morning I will go to receive you in Holy Communion.[40] Dear Jesus, tomorrow, when you are in my heart, think of my soul as an apple. As the apple has black seeds inside, inside my soul is a cupboard. And as inside the apple's black seeds there are white seeds, inside my soul's cupboard is the white seed of your grace. May this grace keep you in me forever and ever.*

Dear Jesus, I know that people make many offenses and I want to make amends for all these offenses. Dear Jesus, if you were alive today, I would shut you away in a house, so that you would not feel the offenses made against you. You could do this! Come into my heart and stay close to me. I will sacrifice a lot for you and say a few little words to comfort you.

Dear Jesus, tell Mary that I know that tomorrow is her feast and that I want to make many sacrifices to comfort her.

Dear Jesus, tell God the Father that I love him very much.

---

[40] Antonietta is referring to the Feast of Our Lady of Fatima, which on February 10, 1937, was on a Thursday.

Dear Jesus, I adore you and I kiss your feet and I send you many blessings.

Your dear,

Antonietta and Jesus

P.S. Dear Jesus, you who suffered so much on the Cross, teach me to do my duty and make many sacrifices.

Letter 135

February 14, 1937

Dear Crucified Jesus,

I love you very much and I adore you greatly. You suffered so much on the Cross. I want to make amends for all the sins that made you suffer. Dear Jesus, I thank you that I could receive you into my heart this morning.[41]

Dear Jesus, tell God the Father and the Holy Spirit that I love them very much and that I ask them and you for the graces necessary to come to Heaven.

Dear Jesus, it has been a few nights since I wrote to you. Forgive me.

Dear Jesus, convert many sinners, save many souls from Purgatory, and bring them to Heaven to glorify the Most Holy Trinity.

Dear Jesus, I want to always be on Calvary under your Cross because you make me always grow better.

Dear Jesus, bless the Church, the Pope, the clergy, my family, and everyone in the world.

Dear Jesus, I adore you at the foot of your Cross and I give you many blessings.

Your dear,

Antonietta and Jesus

P.S. I adore you, Jesus.

---

[41] This date, February 14, 1937, was the First Sunday of Lent.

Letter 136

February 17, 1937

Dear Jesus in the Eucharist,

I adore you greatly and I love you so much!

Dear Jesus, give me a good confession tomorrow.

Dear Jesus, help me with your grace to always be better.

Dear Jesus, save many, many souls and bring them to Heaven to glorify the Most Holy Trinity.

Dear Jesus, I love school a lot. Grant that I'll do well. I entrust to you my teacher. I entrust to you that person whom you know and I entrust to you those who have asked for my prayers. I entrust to you my mommy. Heal her soon for me.

Dear Jesus, forgive many sinners, more than many, and convert them. Dear Jesus, I entrust Spain to you, and all those who died. Bring them to Heaven right away.[42]

Dear Jesus, tell God the Father that I love him very much, and tell him that I also entrust Spain to him.

Dear Jesus, tell the Holy Spirit that I also love him a lot, to illuminate me with his grace, and to make me go to Heaven.

---

[42] Antonietta is likely referring to the Spanish Civil War, namely to the Battle of Jarama. Although the battle lasted for three weeks, during those first ten days, from February 6 - February 15, over 20,000 people died.

Dear Jesus, tell Mary that I want to be near her on Calvary under your Cross.

Dear Jesus, I entrust to you the Church, the Pope and that you heal him, and I entrust to you my confessor, all the clergy, and my family.

Dear Jesus, I adore you, I kiss your feet, and I give you many blessings.

Your dear,

Antonietta and Jesus

P.S. Jesus, I love you and I adore you, O Jesus!

Letter 137

February 21, 1937

Dear Jesus in the Eucharist,

I thank you that I could come to receive you in Holy Communion this morning.[43]

Dear Jesus, make me healthier, save the souls of many sinners, and free many souls from Purgatory.

Dear Jesus, tell God the Father that I love him very much! Dear Jesus, I thank you for giving grace to that person. Dear Jesus, help my teacher, my family, Caterina, and everyone who asks for my prayers.

Dear Jesus, I especially entrust Spain to you.

Dear Jesus, bless the Church, the Holy Father, the clergy, my family, and everyone in the world.

Dear Jesus, I adore you at the foot of your cross.

From your dear

Antonietta

Antonietta and Jesus

---

[43] This date, February 21, 1937, was the Second Sunday of Lent.

March 1, 1937

Dear Jesus in the Eucharist,

Truthfully, today, I was very bad, but tomorrow, dear Jesus, I promise to be much better. Help me to keep this promise and to never disobey the teacher.

Dear Jesus, I know that you have not been happy with me today, but I want to make you happy tomorrow.

Dear Jesus, free many souls from Purgatory and save the souls of many sinners. I also entrust Spain to you.

Dear Jesus, I entrust to you that person whom you know.

Dear Jesus, bless the Church. I very much entrust to you the Holy Father, heal him soon, and make him better. I also entrust to you the clergy and especially my family.

Dear Jesus, I adore you and I want you to be in my heart. Your dear Antonietta gives you many blessings and kisses.

Antonietta and Jesus

Letter 139

Dear Jesus in the Eucharist,

I write to you, dear Jesus, because you make me think of so many beautiful things!

Dear Jesus, I adore you very much and I love you a lot! Give me the souls of many sinners so that they can convert and be with you in Heaven.

Dear Jesus, I am very happy that I am going to confession tomorrow, because the priest represents you, and all my sins will be erased, O Dear Jesus!

Dear Jesus, free many souls from Purgatory so that they go to Heaven to glorify the Trinity. I also entrust Spain to you and everyone in the whole world.

Dear Jesus, tell God the Father that I also adore and love him.

Dear Jesus, tell the Holy Spirit to bless me and to purify me with your love.

Dear Jesus, I want to be beneath your cross, near Mary and near you, and I want to be your lamp that burns day and night before your Sacrament.

Dear Jesus, I entrust to you the Church. Dear Jesus, I entrust to you the Holy Father, the bishops, and all priests, especially my spiritual father.

Dear Jesus, I kiss your wounds and I adore you.
Your dear Antonietta

Sacred Heart of Jesus, I adore you.

Sacred Heart of Jesus, your kingdom come.
Antonietta and Jesus

Letter 140

March 9, 1937

Dear Jesus in the Eucharist,

I really had a tantrum today, but I want to improve tomorrow, dear Jesus. I adore you so much! Dear Jesus, tell God the Father that I also adore him greatly, and also tell him (and I ask you too) to let me go to Heaven.

Dear Jesus, I am very happy to be near you on Calvary. I am very happy that I went to your house today and found you. I promise that I'll be there every day to tell you many beautiful things.

Dear Jesus, I want to be your flower and your lamp. The lamp that burns day and night and never goes out. The flower above the altar, always beautiful, open and never dry. That flower is a lily.

Dear Jesus, I know how much you suffered on the Cross, and I know that your heart was pierced. I want to always be locked inside your heart with you.

Dear Jesus, tell the Holy Spirit that I adore him greatly, tell him to illuminate me and to fill me with his grace.

Dear Jesus, bless the Church, the clergy, and I very much entrust to you my spiritual father and my family.

Dear Jesus, I send you many blessings and kisses.

From your dear

Antonietta and Jesus

P.S. Dear Jesus, I love you.

Letter 141

March 11, 1937

Dear Jesus on the Cross,

Dear Jesus, I know that in a few days it will be Easter, your Resurrection, and that makes me very happy.[44]

Dear Jesus, I want to do your will always. I have always loved you and I will love you forever.

Dear Jesus, I entrust Spain to you. Convert many sinners. Dear Jesus, I entrust to you all the children who have died. Bring them to Heaven right now![45]

---

[44] Easter would happen in two weeks' time, on March 28, 1937.

[45] Antonietta is likely referring to the death of children in Spain. A few months after this date, in May 1937, there was a major evacuation of Spanish children to Britain, Mexico, and Russia, among other countries. However, atrocities against children began months earlier. Irishman Bill Scott, who was in Madrid in December 1936, wrote to the Irish publication, "The Worker," explaining the situation. Published in January 1937, Scott reported: *For the last few days the Fascists have been bombing and shelling the City. They have bombed hospitals and schools. I wouldn't believe it only I have seen it with my own eyes. They have killed hundreds of children, nurses and wounded men. They have deliberately aimed at these hospitals and schools, for they are flying low at the time. Last week thirty planes took part in an air raid. They bombed a tenement house where thirty families lived. You can imagine what happened... Prisoners are seldom taken at all. They don't even shoot them. They kill them with bayonets. That is what they call Christianity... The Fascists kept Xmas Day by a bombardment of*

Dear Jesus, I know that you suffered a lot on the Cross and I want to do many sacrifices to make amends for the sins that made you feel so much pain.

Dear Jesus, I entrust to you the Church, the clergy, especially my spiritual father, my family, and everyone in the whole world.

Dear Jesus, I adore you from the foot of your Cross and I send you many kisses.

Your

Antonietta and Jesus

Madrid, killing women and children! Bill Scott's biography can be found in "Fighting for Republican Spain 1936-38."

Letter 142

March 14, 1937

Dear Jesus on the Cross,

I know that in a few days it will be Easter, the most beautiful feast you have given us, O Jesus, the day when you rose and went to Heaven to sit at the right hand of the Father, who is God.

Dear Jesus, heal me soon, so I can at least go to adore you in the Holy Sepulcher.[46]

Dear Jesus, I will go to confession in a few days. Dear Jesus, I want to receive the Holy Eucharist very soon.

Dear Jesus, I want to stay always locked in your heart. I want to be with you forever.

Dear Jesus, convert many sinners, especially those in Spain.

Dear Jesus, your Antonietta sends you many blessings and kisses.

Antonietta and Jesus

---

[46] This day, March 14, 1937, was the Sunday before Passion Sunday, and two weeks before Easter. Antonietta desires to be well enough by the Triduum, so that she can attend the Good Friday services, celebrating Jesus's death and entombment.

Letter 143

March 15, 1937

Dear Jesus Crucified,

I disobeyed a lot today. Dear Jesus, I ask your forgiveness.

Dear Jesus, I love you so much! Free many souls from Purgatory and save many sinners. Convert them, make them go to confession, and take them to Heaven with you.

Dear Jesus, I love my teacher very much. Help her and bless her.

Letter 144

March 16, 1937

Dear Jesus Crucified,

I adore you, O Dear Jesus! Dear Jesus, tell God the Father that I adore him very much!

Dear Jesus, I am very happy that Holy Easter is coming!

Dear Jesus, I know that you suffered so much on the Cross. I want to suffer with you this Passion Week. I want to suffer for souls who need it, so that they convert.

Dear Jesus, I love you so very, very much, O Jesus, and I want to be your lamp and your lily. The lily represents the purity of the soul. The lamp represents the flame of love that never leaves you alone.

Dear Jesus, bless the Church, the clergy, especially my confessor, my family, my teacher, and everyone in the whole world!

Dear Jesus, many kisses and blessings from your Antonietta and Jesus

Letter 145

Dear Mary Immaculate,

Dear Mary, you are so pure. Make me as pure as you. You have suffered so much these days. I want to endure the Cross with you.

Dear Mary Immaculate, tell Jesus that I love him intensely.

Dear Mary, help me make a good confession tomorrow. Help me remember all my sins. Help me not to do them again. I want to correct all my faults, to be better, and to please Jesus and you, dear Mary.

Dear Mary, I truly love you. Tell the Holy Spirit to enlighten me and bless me.

Dear Mary, tell God the Father that I entrust myself to him and that I love him greatly.

Dear Mary, bless the Church, the clergy, especially my spiritual father, help him in everything he needs. Bless my family and everyone in the whole world.

Dear Mary, receive many blessings and kisses, and tell Jesus that I kiss all his wounds.

Antonietta and Jesus

Letter 146

March 22, 1937

Dear Jesus Scourged,

Dear Jesus, you suffered so much during the scourging for us. O Jesus, you did not deserve to suffer. I acknowledge all my sins and I ask you to forgive me.

Dear Jesus, truly, everyone is very bad. I ask you to forgive my sins, and everyone else's. You are so good. Make them come to Heaven.

Dear Jesus, during the scourging, you suffered so much patiently. I want to learn that. If someone slaps me or disrespects me, I do not have to repay them, but instead I take it good-naturedly for love of you.

Dear Jesus, I offer you all my sacrifices to make amends for every sin that sinners do and will do against you, but help me because without your help I can do nothing.

Dear Jesus, I love you intensely and I want to be near you always. Dear Jesus, I want to be your lamp that burns near you with the flame of love. I want to be the lily that always adorns your altar and adores you.

Dear Jesus, this Holy Week, I want to pray and make little flowers. Dear Jesus, I did not have a tantrum today, so I offer you this little flower I made. Help me to really make many this week to adorn your altar for Easter, O Jesus. You will be risen. And with you in our hearts, love will also have to rise.

Dear Jesus, I want to write a letter to you every night this week. And on Easter Day, I want to write a very beautiful letter.

Dear Jesus, I love you and I kiss your wounds.
Antonietta and Jesus

Letter 147

March 25, 1937

Dear Baby Jesus,

Dear Baby Jesus, when you were small, you obeyed your mommy always. I want to imitate you. Dear Jesus, I want to do many, many, many sacrifices because I love you very, very, very, super, super very much!

Dear Baby Jesus, save many souls. Dear Jesus I want to stay all day every day under your cross and be very good. But without your help, I can do nothing.

Dear Jesus, more than anything, I want to be on Calvary with all my love and doing your will.

Dear Jesus, tell God the Father that I even want to abandon myself into his arms, and yours, so I can safely come to Heaven.

Dear Jesus, many blessings and kisses and caresses from your Antonietta.

Dear Mary, you suffered so very much for your Jesus. Help us to suffer also with such patience.

Antonietta

Letter 148

March 25, 1937

Dear Most Holy Trinity,

Dear God the Father, I love you very, very, very, super very much! The Father's name is really beautiful! When Jesus was on earth, he could not teach us a more beautiful name than this good, loving, charitable Father, who forgives all sinners. What a beautiful name! Father! A good, very good daddy. God the Father, I hope you will love me a lot. I want to be good forever and ever.

Dear Jesus, I love you very, very much. Dear Jesus, I also hope that you will love me so much that you will save many souls from Purgatory so that they go to Heaven to glorify you, dear Jesus. I want to say it again, I love you very, very much!

Dear Holy Spirit, I love you very much. Bless me and illuminate my body and my soul. Dear Holy Spirit, you are the love of the Father and the Son. Sanctify me and help me in all sorrowful suffering.

Kisses,
Antonietta

Letter 149

March 26, 1937

Dear Jesus Crucified,

Today,[47] you died on the Cross for the redemption of sinners. I want to worship you and acknowledge that you suffered for me. I also acknowledge all my sins and I promise to never commit them again.

Dear Jesus, you were in three hours of agony. Your mother was there also. I want to suffer with those pious women and pour out tears of pain.

Dear Jesus, I was sick today and I offered you all my pain.

Dear Jesus, I promise that I will offer to you all the pains you send to me. Make every step a little word of love, dear Jesus.

Dear Jesus, I entrust to you my spiritual director. Help him to preach well and do everything he must do. Also, help my parents.

Blessings and kisses from your dear,
Antonietta

---

[47] This date, March 26, 1937, was Good Friday.

March 28, 1937

Easter

Dear Daddy and Mommy,

Here is my first little letter to tell you of all my love and to wish you many beautiful things today, Easter Day. On this beautiful day, I pray to the Risen Jesus to bless us all and keep you in my love for many, many years.

I promise I'll get well to make you happy.

I kiss you.

Love,

Antonietta

---

[48] This is Antonietta's first personally handwritten letter.

Letter 151

March 30, 1937

Dear Risen Jesus,

I did not write on Easter, but I want to write today and I want it to be a beautiful letter.

Dear Jesus, I adore you intensely and I love you very much. Dear Jesus, I want to do what you want. I want to abandon myself into your hands.

Dear Jesus, heal me so that I can go back to school.

Dear Jesus, save many souls and convert many sinners.

Dear Jesus, tell God the Father that I also entrust to him my healing. Dear Jesus, tell him also that I love him very, very much!

Dear Jesus tell the Holy Spirit to illuminate me, to fill me with his grace, and to bless me.

Dear Jesus, tell Mary to bless me, and that I always want to stay under her mantle, and to pray that you will give me all necessary graces for my soul and body.

Dear Jesus, I want to abandon myself into your hands. Do what you want to me. I want to say again that I really love you very, very much. Dear Jesus, I also want to say again that I entrust souls to you.

Dear Jesus, I want to be under your Cross with you. You suffered so much, and died, and after three days you resurrected. You stayed forty more days with us.

Dear Jesus, I want to be your lamp, the flame that signifies the love of the heart, and your lily that signifies the purity of the soul.

Dear Jesus, I kiss your hands and feet and the Holy Wound of your side. I entrust to you my spiritual director.

I send you many blessings.

Your

Antonietta and Jesus

Letter 153

April 2, 1937

Dear Jesus Crucified,

I adore you greatly.

Dear Jesus, I want to abandon myself into your hands.

Dear Jesus this is my first letter that I am writing to you.[49]

Dear Jesus, I entrust to you the souls of sinners.

Dear Jesus, I entrust to you my parents, my sister, and my spiritual father.

Blessings and kisses,

Antonietta and Jesus

---

[49] Although Antonietta already wrote a letter by hand to her mother and father on Easter, in Letter 150, this is her first time writing a letter to Jesus without her mother's help.

Letter 152[50]

April 3, 1937

Dear Risen Jesus,
I love you a lot.
Dear Jesus, I entrust souls to you. I also entrust to you sinners.
Dear Jesus, help my mommy.
Dear Jesus, I send you so many kisses!
Antonietta and Jesus

---

[50] This is Antonietta's third handwritten letter, and her second letter addressed to Jesus.

Letter 154[51]

April 8, 1937

Dear Jesus in the Eucharist,
Today I came to receive you.[52]
Dear Jesus, I adore you and I love you very much.
Dear Jesus, I entrust sinners to you.
Dear Jesus, I entrust to you my mommy.
Dear Jesus, tell God the Father that I love him.
Dear Jesus, I send you many kisses.
Antonietta and Jesus

---

[51] This is Antonietta's fourth handwritten letter, and her third letter addressed to Jesus.

[52] This date, April 8, 1937, was the Second Thursday of Easter. Antonietta wrote in Letter 128, January 31, 1937, that her mother did not take her to weekday mass. However, as Antonietta's diminishing health became more evident, while her increasing faith also became more evident, her mother arranged for a priest to bring Holy Communion to her daily.

Letter 155

April 9, 1937[53]

Dear Jesus Crucified,

I could not come to Holy Communion today, but I made it spiritually. I believe that you come spiritually if I cannot come personally.

Dear Jesus, I want to be your lamp and your lily that are on the altar.

Dear Jesus, you suffered so much on the Cross. I want to make amends for all the sins that people have committed against you, sins that hurt you still because they make you unhappy.

Dear Jesus, I bless you and I would like to bless everyone.

Dear Jesus, convert sinners so that they go to Heaven. I entrust myself to you.

Dear Jesus, I entrust to you everyone who has asked for my prayers. I also entrust to you my mommy so that she speaks better, my parents, and above all my spiritual father.

Dear Jesus, I desire to see you, and I wish everyone could see you, then, yes, they would love you better.[54]

---

[53] This date, April 9, 1937, was the Second Friday of Easter.

[54] In this letter, Antonietta's mother twice writes "V" for "vederti" (to see you) when taking dictation for Antonietta. In *Carissimo Dio Padre* (2009), Maira Rosaria del Genio suggests that Antonietta did this because she did not want to

Dear Jesus, I kiss all your wounds.
Your
Antonietta and Jesus

---

clearly state that she sees Jesus. In this translation, rather than demonstrating Antonietta's humility by writing only "V", the translator has inserted the intent of her words, to show that Antonietta desires to *see* Jesus, and that she wishes everyone could *see* him too.

Letter 156

Dear Great Jesus,

Dear Jesus, I love you very, very much! Dear Jesus, I want to be a saint and I want to make many sacrifices, but you must help me, because without your help I can do nothing.

Dear Jesus, I entrust to you the souls of many sinners, and I entrust to you also the sinner whom you know. Dear Jesus, I entrust to you also the souls of the poor dead, especially my grandfather, Antonio, if he did not go to Heaven, and also my other grandfather, Giovanni.

Dear Jesus, I wish there were no school holidays. I wish I never got sick. I wish I could come visit you all day in the sisters' church. Instead, unfortunately, I am always ill. Heal me so that I do not get sick anymore.

Dear Jesus, how happy I am to be your lamp and your lily, the lamp that is the flame of love, the lily that is the purity of the soul, both on the altar to adore you. That beautiful flower is me, who adores you! These two keep you company always, the lamp burning day and night, the lily wanting to worship you forever and ever!

Dear Jesus, tell God the Father that I love him very, very much, and that I bless him.

Dear Jesus, tell the Holy Spirit to illuminate me with his grace and fill me with his seven gifts.

Dear Jesus, tell Mary that I love her very much. Make my soul like hers.

Dear Jesus, I send you a lot of blessings and kisses.

Your

Antonietta of Jesus

P.S. I entrust to you my spiritual father.

Letter 157[55]

April 18, 1937

Dear Jesus in the Eucharist,

I came to see you in church today. Dear Jesus, I love you very, very much! Dear Jesus, I want to be a nun. Dear Jesus, I ask you to forgive all my sins.

Dear Jesus, I entrust to you all sinners.

Dear Jesus, I entrust to you my parents.

Dear Jesus, I entrust to you the clergy, my spiritual father, my family, and everyone in the world.

Many kisses,

Antonietta and Jesus

---

[55] This is Antonietta's fifth and final handwritten letter, and her fourth and final letter addressed to Jesus. However, she recommences writing diary entries on the following week, on April 26, 1937 (Diary Entry 4), addressing them also to God and Mary. There has not been a diary entry for almost seven months exactly, not since September 27, 1936.

Letter 158

April 21, 1937

Dear Baby Jesus,

I was very bad today. Forgive me. I promise that I won't be bad anymore like today. Maybe tomorrow I can go to my spiritual father. Help me to make a good confession.

Dear Jesus, help me to be good because without your help I cannot do anything. Anything!

Dear Jesus, I entrust to you my spiritual father, the clergy, and everyone in the whole world.

Dear Jesus, I will write you a beautifully long letter on April 25.

Dear Jesus, many blessings and kisses from your Antonietta.

Antonietta of Jesus

Letter 159

April 25, 1937[56]

Dear Jesus in the Eucharist,

Today, O Dear Jesus, I re-offer the sacrifice of my leg.

Dear Jesus, firstly, thank you for all the ways that you have given another day for us to come nearer to you in Heaven. Secondly, thank you for the strength you have given us to bear our cross patiently. Thirdly, I thank you because I received First Communion this year and you came to live in my heart. What a feast for me that day! It was the most beautiful day of my life.

Dear Jesus, thank you also for giving me a good report card.

Dear Jesus, I want to be good always, but this morning I did my homework wrong, and I ask your forgiveness. I ask you, Forgive me!

Dear Jesus, I want to always be your lamp and your lily that adores you. It would make me happy to be your lamp. I hope it will make you happy, too.

---

[56] This day marks the one-year anniversary of the amputation of Antonietta's leg. Because she had made so many little sacrifices throughout the year, offering up to Jesus all the pains that this amputation had caused her, Antonietta believed it was very important to celebrate the gift of her leg to the Lord, which she viewed as an opportunity to suffer for the glory of God and the salvation of souls.

Dear Jesus, I have not seen you at all in several days. But let me see you again because I love you so much! Today, I want to see you only!

How painful were these days this year! But I have born them all for you, dear Jesus. You saved many souls. I want to save so many more today.

I entrust to you my parents, my sister, especially my spiritual father, all the clergy, and the Holy Father.

Dear God the Father, I thank you as I thanked Jesus because you are infinitely good!

Dear Holy Spirit, illuminate me and fill me with all seven gifts. Dear Holy Spirit, I also thank you as I thanked Jesus.

Dear Mary, thanks also to you. I thank you, O dear Mary!

Dear Jesus, I kiss your wounds.

Your Antonietta

Antonietta of Jesus

Letter 160

April 26, 1937

Dear Holy Spirit,

Dear Holy Spirit, in a few days, I will receive the Sacrament of Confirmation. I desire you so very much that I cannot wait for the day! Give me all seven of your gifts, illuminate me, fill me with your grace, and sanctify me.

Dear Holy Spirit, you are the love that unites the Father and the Son. Unite me also to the Most Holy Trinity.

Dear Holy Spirit, tell Jesus that I love him very, very much. Tell God the Father that I praise him and bless him.

Dear Holy Spirit, blessings and kisses from your dear,

Antonietta of Jesus

Diary Entry 4

April 26, 1937

Dear Holy Spirit, in a few days I will receive you.

Diary Entry 5

April 27, 1937

Most Holy Trinity, I love you very much!
Dear Holy Spirit, illuminate me and sanctify me.
Dear Holy Spirit, bless me.

Diary Entry 6

April 28, 1937

Dear Holy Spirit, you who unites the Father and the Son, unite with me also.

Diary Entry 7

April 29, 1937

Dear Holy Spirit, when you come into my heart, fill me with your seven gifts and your love.

Dear Holy Spirit, I want to be better tomorrow.

Diary Entry 8

April 30, 1937

Dear Holy Spirit, on the day that I receive you, I want to make many small sacrifices.

Diary Entry 9

May 1, 1937

Dear Holy Spirit, I want to obey always.

Letter 161

May 2, 1937

Dear Mary,

I love you so much and I want to do many little sacrifices for you this month.[57]

Dear Mary, tell God the Father that I love him very much!

Dear Mary, also tell your son Jesus that I am happy that he came into my heart today. Dear Mary, tell the Holy Spirit that I am very happy that in a few days I will receive him and that I will be very happy to receive him!

Dear Mary, help me go to Heaven to be with Jesus, all the saints, and also with you.[58] Dear Mary, I want to say again that I love you so very, very much! Through Jesus, help me save many souls, oh, so many, many souls!

---

[57] The month of May is traditionally dedicated to honoring Mary, beginning with the May Crowning on May 1st.

[58] This date, May 2, 1937, was the sixth and final Sunday of Easter. Antonietta's final feasts in this world would celebrate Ascension Sunday on the following week, Pentecost on the Sunday after that, the Solemnity of the Holy Trinity on the Sunday after that, and the Solemnity of Corpus Christi on the Sunday after that. However, she would die three days before the next Sunday, the Solemnity of the Sacred Heart of Jesus, yet she undoubtedly celebrated that feast in Heaven, where her own holy heart would be united to Our Lord's.

Dear Mary, tell the Holy Spirit to illuminate me, to give me all seven gifts, to make me holy, and to make me grow in goodness.

Dear Mary, I entrust to you the Church, the Holy Father, the clergy, and especially my spiritual father. I also entrust to you my family, and especially my parents. I entrust to you Aunt Laurina, all my grandparents, my aunts and uncles, my relatives, and everyone.

Blessings and kisses from your dear Antonietta, Antonietta of Jesus

Diary Entry 10

May 2, 1937

Dear Holy Spirit, I am happy today because I have received Jesus. For the merits of Jesus, give me your seven gifts.

Dear Mary, this month, I want to make many small sacrifices.

Diary Entry 11

May 3, 1937[59]

Dear Holy Spirit, I want to give you many small sacrifices today.

---

[59] This date, May 3, 1937, was a Monday and the Feasts of the Apostles, Saints Phillip and James.

Diary Entry 12

May 4, 1937

Dear Holy Spirit, tell Jesus that I want to be his lamp and I want to be his lily.

Diary Entry 13

May 5, 1937

Dear Holy Spirit, fill me with your grace, and help me make many small sacrifices, to prepare me to receive you worthily.

Diary Entry 14

May 6, 1937[60]

Dear Holy Spirit, tell Jesus, who ascended into Heaven today, to let our souls also ascend to Heaven one day.

---

[60] This date, May 6, 1937, was Thursday, the fortieth day after Easter, the Feast of the Ascension of Our Lord.

Diary Entry 15

May 7, 1937

Dear Holy Spirit, I want you to be my Spirit of Love, too.

Diary Entry 16

May 8, 1937

Dear Holy Spirit, I want to make so many little sacrifices that I make you happy when you enter into my heart.

Diary Entry 17

May 9, 1937

Dear Holy Spirit, tell Mary that I love her very much!

Diary Entry 18

May 10, 1937

Dear Holy Spirit, fill me with your grace and make me love you always.

Diary Entry 19

May 11, 1937

Dear Holy Spirit, I know that I will receive you in a few days. I want to love you more and more!

Diary Entry 20

May 12, 1937

Dear Holy Spirit, I want to make you happy always. When you enter into my heart, I want you to find it white and pure.

Diary Entry 21

May 13, 1937

Dear Mary, help me to have a good Confirmation. I want to know you, my Heavenly Mommy.

Diary Entry 22

May 14, 1937

Dear Holy Spirit, tomorrow I will receive you. I am very happy, and I will be a Soldier of God.

Written Essay 1

May 18, 1937

In the fields of my heart, new fruits of goodness sprout.

Lord, protect me. Keep every danger away from me. Evil does not spoil the good sown in me during this school year, which is almost finished.

Written Essay 2

May 18, 1937

May blooms flowers. May is the month of Mary.
Mommy is so helpful.

Letter 162[61]

June 2, 1937

Dear Jesus Crucified,

I love you very much and I adore you!

I want to be on Calvary with you and suffer with joy because of the knowledge that I am on Calvary.

Dear Jesus, thank you for sending me this illness because it is a way to go to Heaven.

Dear Jesus, tell God the Father that I also love him very much.

Dear Jesus, I want to be your lamp and your lily, dear Jesus.

Dear Jesus, give me the necessary strength to bear this pain for sinners.[62]

Dear Jesus, tell the Holy Spirit to illuminate me with love and to fill me with all seven gifts.

Dear Jesus, tell Mary that I love her very much and that I want to be together with her on Calvary because I want to be your victim of love, dear Jesus.

Dear Jesus, I entrust to you my spiritual father. Give him all necessary graces.

---

[61] This letter marks Antonietta's final written words to Jesus.

[62] Right when Antonietta prays to bear pain for sinners, she has to vomit. Her mother immediately takes her away. But when Antonietta returns, she continues dictating the letter to her mother.

Dear Jesus, I entrust to you my parents and Margherita.

Dear Jesus, I send you many blessings and kisses.

Antonietta of Jesus

Antonietta Meo fell gravely ill a week after dictating her final letter. Her breathing became labored; fluid was building in her lungs. On June 23, her parents brought her to S. Stefano Rotondo's Clinic where the doctors made incisions along her ribs to remove the fluid. Maria Meo's memoir records how, when Antonietta saw Maria weeping uncontrollably, she looked at her mother tenderly and tried to comfort her with the words, "Be happy, mommy. Be happy... I will be leaving in about ten days." Hearing this, her father called their priest, who came to administer the Anointing of the Sick. The priest asked Antonietta, "Do you know what this holy oil is?" She told him that it is a sacrament given to the dying. "It also helps people recover," he tried to explain, but at these words, she refused to receive the sacrament because she did not want to diminish her suffering for Jesus. When the priest explained to her that the holy oil also increases grace, Antonietta stretched out her hands and said, "I want it!"

Ten days later, on July 3, 1937, exactly the day Antonietta had prophesied, her final hours were spent at home and in bed, surrounded by her family. Early in the morning, she opened her eyes and saw a vision of St. Thérèse of Lisieux. The dying child told her heavenly intercessor that she wanted to stay longer and suffer more, but St. Thérèse said, "It is enough." Thus, a month and a day after her last letter, at the age of six years old, Antonietta's final words were gentle whispers: "Jesus… Mary… Mommy… Daddy…" She smiled and made a long sigh, then she left for Heaven.

Pope Benedict XVI gave her the title Venerable in 2007, which also commenced her process for canonization. On the day she is canonized, she will be the youngest saint confessor in the Church's history. Only two miracles are needed for her canonization.

Antonietta was buried in the Basilica di Santa Croce in Gerusalemme, in Rome, her family's parish where Antonietta received her sacraments, and where she could also be heard whispering to the tabernacle, "Jesus, come out and play with me!"

Venerable Antonietta Meo,
pray for us!